Actor Training 3

Smith

Ross

Sommer

Hart

Richard P. Brown, editor

Institute for Acting Research with

Drama Book Specialists (Publishers)

Actor Training 3

CONTRIBUTORS

LINDA SMITH has studied theatre and dance at the University of Minnesota and the University of Utah with Dr. John M. Wilson and voice with Kristin Linklater and Arthur Strimling. She has taught, choreographed and directed. Her vision is of a theatre where actors move with the power of dancers and dancers speak with the power of actors, not as a weak compromise but as a form with the communicative strength of both.

DUNCAN ROSS began his career as a professional actor in England with the Royal Shakespeare Company, the Old Vic Theatre Center and other companies. He became the general administrator of the Birmingham Playhouse and the Director of the Old Vic Theatre School, Bristol. In the United States, he founded the professional training program for actors at the University of Washington. Currently he is Artistic Director of the Seattle Repertory Theatre.

SALLY R. SOMMER has written articles on dance and theatre for The Drama Review, Encyclopedia of Dance and Ballet and other publications. She is on the theatre faculty of C. W. Post College and is currently working on a book about Loie Fuller.

JOSEPH HART is a playwright, actor, director and member of the faculty of the Theatre Arts Department of Rutgers University. He has had several of his plays published and six Equity showcases in New York City. In recent years he has been founder-director of the N. Y. U. Drama Society, The Melting Pot Repertory and The Rutgers Theatre Arts Experimental Workshop. He is currently at work on a new full-length play.

CONTENTS

VOICE, MOVEMENT AND THE IRIS WARREN METHOD

LINDA C. SMITH

INTRODUCTION

All art forms are physicalizations of man's feelings for himself and his environment. Each art form has its own model, mode and medium. [1]

In the theatre the model is man himself. Every play deals with man's acts. The total structure of human acts creates the mode of theatre. By human acts we mean <u>any</u> act which man does. [2] The primary medium of theatre is the human body. Physicalization is the primary focus of the actor. As Viola Spolin has put it:

> A player can dissect, analyze, intellectualize or develop
> a valuable history for his part, but if he is unable to assim-
> ilate it and communicate it physically, it is useless within
> the theatre form. [3]

Too often we are mystified by the personal creative process of single actors. At least we have ceased to believe that acting is such a complex human activity that it cannot be analyzed. I do not believe that it is possible to ever fully understand the creative process that <u>each</u> individual must go through. We must be sensitive to the differences, but we need to search for the common ground of mutual creativity. Again, as Spolin puts it:

> Nor need we be concerned with the feelings of the actor,
> for use in the theatre. We should be interested only in his
> direct physical communications. His feelings are personal
> to him. [4]

The physical process of which Ms. Spolin writes is not so concealed, elusive or "mystical" as the individual creative process. The physical process is the basis for the actor's experience within the theatre.

It is the medium by which the audience experiences theatre. Jerzy Grotowski has stressed this aspect of the theatre:

> A man in an elevated spiritual state uses rhythmically articulate signs, <u>begins to dance to sing.</u> A sign not a common gesture is the <u>elementary integer</u> of expression for us. [5]

This paper will deal with the physical process which is the basis for 1) the actor's medium of expression and 2) the actor's experience as an artist within the theatre. The paper is divided into two major areas: 1) The Actor's Medium and 2) The Actor's Experience. While these two areas are inseparable in the immediate work of an actor, we may examine each separately. Beginning with an examination of the Iris Warren method of voice production, we can define and analyze the actor's medium and discover how we can approach the actor's experience.

The concept behind any method of acting is the disciplined and orderly exploration of the human body and its environment. The Iris Warren method of voice production is centered on just such an exploration. The method is rooted in the exploration and development of the actor's medium, the body, and the actor's experience within the theatre. In both theory and practice the Iris Warren method treats experience and physical process as inseparable.

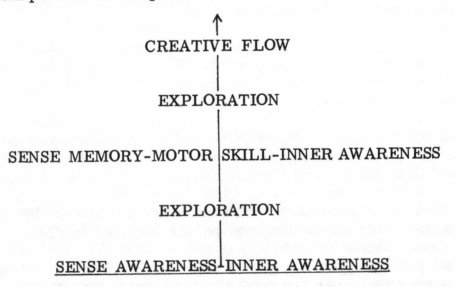

CREATIVE FLOW

↑

EXPLORATION

SENSE MEMORY-MOTOR SKILL-INNER AWARENESS

EXPLORATION

<u>SENSE AWARENESS-INNER AWARENESS</u>

THE ACTOR'S MEDIUM

Iris Warren observed that instead of reflecting an organic response to a text, actors often manipulated the voice as though it were "outside the body," attempting to affect the feeling. She believed that the voice could become a direct expression of an organic response. This direct expression could be extraordinarily subtle, filled with power and nuance without any damage to the vocal mechanism.[6] Her method attempts to free the voice to respond to the feeling of a text, making the voice a direct expression of that feeling.

The actor's medium must be responsive to every experience and every experience must be reflected through his medium. Quite simply, Iris Warren recognized that the body was equally a sensory organ and an organ of response.

The freeing of the voice is accomplished by increasing the sense awareness of the body and specifically the awareness of the vocal mechanism. The method attempts to bring the student into sensory contact with his own rhythm and breathing mechanism. It teaches the student to "feel" his tensions and then to release them. He then increases his motor skills (flexibility of the tongue, coordination of the lips, development of a strong and flexible soft palate and so on).

Through sense awareness, the development of the student's perceptions and motor skills, he becomes more aware of himself as a creative human being. With this inner awareness and with the development of the sense awareness he gains "sense memory," which he can use to improve his vocal production and release himself into a text. With the growth of sense awareness, sense memory, motor skills and the inner awareness of himself, he can respond more freely -- spontaneously -- to a text and establish a creative flow.

We will deal with inner awareness, expressiveness and the need to express a bit later. Let us focus here on the actor's medium -- the body -- as a sensory organ and an organ of response.

The idea that man is one physical and psychological unity has been widely explored today. Iris Warren's observations have been supported by modern psychological and physiological theories. Gestalt psychology is of particular interest to anyone exploring the idea of this unity. In Gestalt theory, self awareness, particularly of the organic functioning of the body, is of major importance in finding a balance in a human being. Fritz Perls has outlined in simple language some major aspects of Gestalt therapy:

> A living organism is an organism which consists of thousands of processes that require interchange with other media outside the boundary of the organism.... We touch, we get in contact, we stretch our boundary out to the thing in question. If we are rigid and can't move, then it remains there. When we live, we spend our energies, we need energies to maintain this machine. This process of exchange is called metabolism. Both the metabolism of the exchange of our organism with the environment, and the metabolism within our organism is going on continually, day and night.[7]

Perls links "interchange" with perception. We use our senses for physical survival, as tools to reach outside our own selves in order to

3

exist. Von Buddenbrock put it this way:

> The outside world -- the world perceived by the senses
> -- is the source of all that a form of life is and does,
> thinks and feels.... It [sensory perception] enables the
> organism to meet actively the forces which operate in
> its world. No matter how great the variety of responses
> with which an organism meets its world, we shall be safe
> in saying that all those responses are beneficial to the
> organism. This is the very foundation of the existence of
> every living creature. [8]

Sensory perception is the major tool which the actor uses to make
contact with his environment and other participants.

SELF-EXPERIENCE

Rudolph Arnheim wrote:

> Human thinking, perceptual as well as intellectual, seeks
> the causes of happenings as near to the place of their ef-
> fects as possible. [9]

The actor must become fully aware of himself through his sensory perception. He must begin to turn into himself and become aware
of his physical responses to his own organism as well as to his sur-
roundings. It is the aim of both modern dance technique and the Iris
Warren method to deal with these physical responses and seek to improve the actor's sensory perception.
Let us relate self-awareness again to our organism's own inner
survival system. As Perls said:

> Let us assume that I walk through the desert and its very
> hot. I lose, let's say, eight ounces of fluid. Now, how
> do I know that I lost this? First, through self-awareness
> of the phenomenon, in this case called thirst. [10]

The actor is using inner sensory perception not merely to understand that he is thirsty, but as a tool to discover his own rhythm, his
own expenditure of energy, his own physical reactions to other people,
his whole environment and his own self-image. In a real sense our
brain is locked in a totally dark and soundless world. When stimulation
from the senses -- eyes, ears, nerve impulses from muscle groups
and so forth -- is reduced, the brain will begin to hallucinate. The
cortex begins to create its own reality when its sensory channels are
cut off.

Using the knowledge that reality lies in our own body and is experienced through our own senses, the actor can begin to trust and discover for himself. Instead of seeking outside means he can begin to stimulate and expand himself. This is an essential element of the development of the creative flow. The work of Perls encourages the use of this fearsome freedom:

> So we have come to the most important and interesting phenomenon in all pathology: self-regulation versus external regulation. The anarchy which is usually feared by the controllers is not an anarchy which is without meaning. On the contrary, it means the organism is left alone to take care of itself without being meddled with from outside.... And I believe that this is the great thing to understand: that awareness per se -- by and of itself -- can be a curative.... We can rely on the wisdom of the organism. [11]

Self-regulation is related directly to the Iris Warren method. Instead of manipulating the voice to create an expression, the actor allows the voice to respond to the body -- the physical reactions. The voice becomes a direct expression of the actor's feelings. With the proper guidance the student regulates his own development. As he becomes more aware, more coordinated and stronger, the student can move away from his own problems in a natural way.

We now have the three principles which are essential to understanding and working with the Warren approach:

1) self-awareness of one's own physical phenomena
2) self-regulation (versus external regulation)
3) self-awareness as curative.

THE WARREN APPROACH

What is sense awareness? What senses must we be aware of and why? What motor skills are essential for the actor in a performance? And what does "inner awareness" mean?

The first three questions center around the human body and the physical communication that we linked both to the actor's experience in the theatre and to the audience's experience of the actor.

In 1938 Margret H'Doubler studied the elements contributing to dance; her analysis was based upon the human body. She divided what every student brings to dance into three areas:

1) Anatomical structure
2) Physiological determinants
3) Psychical equipment.

Within these areas we can begin to define sense awareness, motor skills and inner awareness.

In the first area, anatomical structure, we can begin to define what the human body is capable of doing. That is, how it moves. H'Doubler defined the process in this way:

> Anatomical structure sets mechanical limits for motor response. The body is capable of flexion, extension, adduction, abduction, rotation, circumduction, range and the activities of locomotion-walk-run-leap-hop-jump-simple combinations skip-gallop-slide. Their combinations offer an infinite variety of postures, gestures and actions. [12]

Anatomical structure also sets limits upon the vocal mechanism. The voice produces sound. The production of the sound -- the quality the mechanism creates -- is determined by the duration of the vibration, the rapidity of the vibrations and the amplitude of the vibrations.

The vocal mechanism produces hissing, explosions, friction noise and sonorous tones. Varying the time length, the pitches of the sound and the intensity, an infinite number of qualities can be produced. The actor can experiment and develop awareness of the duration of his sounds, his pitches and his intensity to improve and widen the quality of his voice.

Sense awareness and motor skills deal first with the limitations of the human body: the movements it can make and the sounds that it can produce.

1) The actor must become aware that he can make the movements and the sounds.
2) He must develop a continuing awareness of how he produces these movements and sounds.
3) The actor begins through the development of certain specific motor skills to expand the movements and sounds that his body can make. He works to develop more precisely the skills he can already execute.

Here then is the first part of the technique: development of self-awareness of one's own physical phenomena.

The second part of the awareness of physical phenomena is more difficult to work with and to pinpoint. As H'Doubler says:

> Physiological determinants of movements are a consideration of physio-chemical processes and the neuro-muscular system. It is a behavior equipment possessing reflex paths and infinite possible activities that can be modified. It is by virtue of this structure that specific technical skills can be emancipated from diffuse responses. It is highly

modifiable and must be educated by doing.[13]

Quite simply, as the actor begins to develop his sense awareness and works with motor skill he must realize that not only is he re-
training his muscular system but he is re-training his nervous system
and his process of thinking and perceiving. Mary Corrigan has com-
mented on this aspect of the work:

> This method [Iris Warren] depends on the very slow pro-
> cess of developing a kind of "prelogic" thinking where
> the student learns to feel when something is right; he learns
> intuitively to trust what he says and does in relation to
> the feelings which the text evokes within him.[14]

This development of trust in one's own organism is achieved
by the same re-education of the neuro-muscular system that allows
us to overcome brain damage. It is the same system which allows us
to adapt physically to a severe physical injury. It is the reflex system which allows us to move and breathe and react without the use of
our brain. As Corrigan put it:

> [The actor] learns to react immediately and organically
> to signals, (feelings) which are generated far below the
> conscious level of his brain. It is absolutely essential
> that he no longer "think" about what he is doing. This
> method is not based on logical or pragmatic thought,
> where the actor conceptually decides beforehand which
> physical and vocal actions he is going to undertake: What
> the Warren method is really concerned with is the exis-
> tential NOW -- what happens at this very moment. This
> method seeks a spontaneously organic response to the text
> from the whole person: it seeks an immediate and intuitive
> response which is not hampered by intellectualizing.[15]

This process is not "mystical" or "spiritually based." The organic response is made up of the simple reflex actions of the neuro-
muscular system; the proprioceptor sense system and the simple
judgments which we make with our eyes, ears, semi-circular canals,
nose and mouth. All these systems operate continually under the conscious activity of the brain centers. Now our language and conceptual-
ization process has overlaid our organic responses so much that we
mistrust our most accurate means of dealing with the world. Arnheim
observed:

> The delicate balance of all our powers -- which permits
> us to live fully and to work well -- is upset, not only when
> the intellect interferes with intuition, but also when feeling

7

dislodges reasoning.... Language is no avenue for sensory contact with reality -- it serves merely to name what we have seen or heard or thought. [16]

A balance is needed, with full trust of the senses as tools to contact reality, yet using language and intellect to label and interpret those experiences. This is the balance that every actor must seek to grasp. H'Doubler does not slight the mental process at all:

Mental equipment determines psychic behavior. Here resides the awareness of all sensations as well as the capacity to think, feel, imagine, create, etc. It is the equipment for interpreting experience and developing a sense of values. This structure is the informative substance from which emerges personality. It is highly modifiable and educable and needs broad experience. It represents the personal human endowments that through knowledge and use are the only forces that lend warmth and significance to any act. [17]

This is the equipment which creates in the individual "inner awareness." Inner awareness is a combination of the individual's intellectual and physical knowledge of his own organism. It is the knowledge of the process of creating and thinking and perceiving that the individual must go through. This is the center in which all experience is interpreted and labeled. We transfer what we perceive into concepts there. This is where self-regulation and the curative process are formulated and put into use.

It is this combination of elements in every human being through which any technique of acting must develop. These elements are the objective grounds on which personal knowledge and growth must occur. These elements are the foundation for a workable relationship between actor and actor or actor and director. These elements make up the medium of the theatre: the actor.

THE ACTOR'S EXPERIENCE

To develop a sensitive and responsive organism -- that is, to improve the actor's medium -- we must deal with three areas: 1) anatomical structure and its limitations; 2) the physiological determinants or the neuro-muscular system and the organism's perceptual devices; and 3) the mental equipment or analytical and imaginative processes of the individual. When Grotowski spoke of "going beyond yourself," he was talking about the sensitive process of strengthening, stretching and learning how our body works. The training he speaks of encompasses all three elements which create the actor's medium:

8

When I say "go beyond yourself" I am asking for an insupportable effort. One is obliged not to stop despite fatigue and to do things that we know well we cannot do. That means one is also obliged to be courageous. What does this lead to? There are certain points of fatigue which break the control of the mind, a control that blocks us. When we find the courage to do things that are impossible, we make the discovery that our body does not block us. (We do the impossible, we make the discovery that our body doesn't block us.) We do the impossible and the division within us between conception and the body's ability disappears. This attitude, this determination, is a training for how to go beyond our limits. These are not the limits of our nature, but those of our discomfort. These limits we impose upon ourselves that block the creative process, because creativity is never comfortable.[18]

The key to this approach to training is clearly defined by Grotowski's statement: "We do the impossible and the division between conception and the body's ability disappears."

Art as a human creation must not have a dogmatic set of rules and a single vision of what life consists of nor a formula to create an expression of its content. All that any technique can achieve is the freeing of students so they can create with their full potentiality. Mere body conditioning, manipulation of the breathing process or a few stage tricks do not create an actor. To quote Grotowski:

Creativity, especially where acting is concerned, is boundless sincerity, yet disciplined: i.e. articulated signs. The creator should not therefore find his material a barrier in this respect. And as the actor's material is his own body, it should be trained to obey, to be pliable, to respond passively to psychic impulses as if it did not exist during the moment of creation -- by which we mean it does not offer any resistance. Spontaneity and discipline are the basic aspects of an actor's work.... A creative act of quality flourishes only if nourished by the living organism.[19]

The experience any art form provides is an indivisible one. The depth of content is reflected within the uniqueness of its form. Theatre as an art form creates an environment in which actors and spectators arrive at new perceptions of their own experiences.

Art seeks to unify man with his environment. As an artist, an actor seeks unification with the insight into his own being, into his environment and into the being of others. He desires to explore the art to which he has committed himself. In exploring the art, he must explore and expand himself. As Stanley Burnshaw has said:

9

Regardless of what any poem may happen to be "about," all the resemblance-making actions begin and end with unification.... We may even conceive of these unifications of poetry as comprising a generic mode of love. This would be doing the kind of thing that Plato, Jean Baptiste Lacordaire and Freud have done in attributing its multiform manifestations (love of woman, of parents, of a cause, etc., etc.) to a single generative force. For the Greek philosopher, it was mind; for the French theologian, love of God; for the Viennese psychoanalyst, instinctual impulse. To conceive of each poem as "an act of thinking love" implies an even vaster emotion, one which takes these three great forces as themselves but partial expressions of man's organic desire for reunion with creation itself. [20]

Broadening Burnshaw's idea, let us assume that the theatre as an expression is caused by "man's organic desire for reunion with creation itself." To understand this implication is to see the profound possibilities for exploration and expression within its form. If every actor "felt" that the playwright's ultimate purpose was an act of unification, his physical creation would become a search for that unity and that positive expression.

Thus theatre requires commitment, a total physical and mental concentration bringing the reality of the total being into the creative act. The experience the Warren approach tries to provide is the expansion of the actor's body. Learning to trust physical, organic impulses is essential to the development of his art. To trust the natural breathing process, to trust the tension-free state and allow the organic responses to achieve physical form shared with others is a deeply penetrating process -- always gradual and often terrifying.

To begin to mold and expand the actor's experiences any technique must be developed out of these central perceptions:

1) The process of work must evolve out of the three basic elements composing the actor's medium: anatomical structure, physiological processes and mental processes. Working constantly out of the principles of generalization and transfer, the exercises must either work with the elements simultaneously or in sequence.

2) The method should begin with awareness and the development of strength in the anatomical structure and the physiological determinants. The approach begins with the actor's sensitivity to basic physical phenomena.

3) The development within the actor of a total sense of involvement -- discipline -- and the sense of spontaneity.

The approach will then encompass the following sensory experiences:

1) the rhythm of the respiratory cycle;
2) awareness of excessive muscle tensions;
3) the sensation of release of muscle tensions;
4) the most relaxed, natural and beneficial alignment;
5) the sensation of strengthening, stretching, contracting, agility and movement of the muscle groups within the body;
6) the sensation of an economical and easy flow of energy -- psychic and physical;
7) awareness of resonators and of the vibrations of sound waves through the body;
8) awareness of the articulators coordinated, strengthened and flexible;
9) organic response to character, situation, space rhythm, shape and language within the theatrical situation.

Number nine not only includes the basic response of the actor to the text or theatrical situation, but introduces the form factors present in all performances:

1) balance
2) shape
3) form
4) growth
5) space
6) light
7) color
8) movement
9) tension
10) expression [21]

These elements are included constantly within any situation. It is the actor's responsibility to use them and sense them rather than allow them to be accidental.

What follows is a general outline of a work pattern combining voice work with movement in an integrated and organic way.

THE PHYSICAL PHENOMENON OF BREATHING
SENSE AWARENESS

A.   Sense of Rhythm and Capacity of Breathing Process

B.   Sense of General Body Areas

     Back: shoulder girdle; spine, lumbar region; musculature of back

Neck: spinal column; occipital joint, muscle structure

Torso: abdominal muscles, superficial and deep; musculature of chest/ribcage and so forth.

Arms: bone structure; hands; fingers

Head: scalp; bone structure

Face: nose, jaw, eye sockets, bone structure and musculature.

We begin with the simplest and most diffused perceptions:

1.   Skin surface and tactile sensation
2.   Large muscle groups and how they generalize tension and relaxation
3.   Skeletal support: spinal column, shoulders, pelvis, center of gravity, with special attention to the lower back
4.   Specific tension areas varied with the individual
5.   An effortless stance and development of full-length alignment.

C.   Specific Tension Areas
Muscle hanger of the shoulder girdle
The muscles of the neck
The occipital joint
Jaw
Diaphragm
Musculature of the abdomen and lower back

These are some of the areas which carry certain degrees of tension all the time. They are the areas which generalize and from which the body as a whole generalizes tension. These tensions all make the breathing process inadequate and inflexible. The body is usually out of tonus, immobile and weak. With these tensions present, the relaxation and full-capacity of the breathing process can never be fully attained, nor can any real sense of the activities of muscles, joints or the perceptual tools.

D.   Sense of body alignment
Effortless stance
Full- stretch and strength
Sense of space which the body occupies
Full action (to individual potentiality) of flexible spine

E.   Sense of full skeletal support
Support and strength of the musculature of the abdomen and the back
Full length of the thoracic cage

F.   Sense of articulators and resonators
       Lips
       Tongue
       Hard palate
       Soft palate
       Teeth
       Nasal cavity
       Oral cavity
       Sinuses
       Head-skull
       Chest
       Pharynx-larynx

The twentieth century has created an animal beset with hyper-tensions, weak or insensitive muscles and a stooped posture. Weak lower abdominal muscles throw the pelvis forward; the lumbar muscles suffer atrophy and the shoulder girdle becomes weak, losing full width and openness. This posture compresses the thorax and viscera, hindering the ability of the person to draw a full breath. The alignment weakens specific muscles which are essential to full breathing: the lumbar muscles, the rectus abdominis, the obliquus internus and externus, and the transversus thoracis. All these muscles are important in the active process of exhalation. In a weakened state and with inadequate posture, the thorax can not rise to its full height and exhalation is, therefore, superficial. In this condition man experiences varying degrees of muscle tensions. He receives his oxygen through an altered and ineffective process. The body is not nourished properly. Man compensates by attempting to rearrange muscle functions. The shoulders and neck take on tension in an effort to support the erect body, and the lumbar muscles and other back muscles atrophy.

In our culture man becomes unaware of his body, and his muscles lack tone and are unresponsive. Lack of sensation and strength in the human body are also factors in the inadequate functioning of what would be a natural breathing process. The body simply cannot be fully expressive in this state of numbness and insensibility.

The approach to training should be a full integration of experiences which strengthen, make flexible, give quality and coordination to the body and work with specific motor skills and perceptions.

Sense awareness is curative if it serves as a guide to understanding the problems, weaknesses and blocks an actor may have. It can give him confidence in the areas that he is strong in, but it is not a miracle cure.

From these awarenesses the actor must develop an orderly and disciplined program of experiences which enliven, strengthen and explore as fully as possible the three elements of his medium. This is not merely a program of "calisthenics." Every exercise should be approached with the goal of discovery in mind. Conditioning is not a means to creativity, but a responsive body can be the tool in reaching the level of heightened awareness and readiness which makes total creativity possible.

Sense awareness as a guide seems to work on two simple principles: generalization and transfer. The first principle is always at work in the body. If one develops a tension in the neck (whether the source is improper body tonus or mental strain), the body will tend to generalize that feeling and carry the tightness through the whole body. The diaphragm may tighten, the abdominal muscles may be stiff, the neck may become inflexible, the jaw may clench the teeth. All these reactions will cause improper breathing, lack of powerful exhalation, poor articulation, stiffness of movement throughout the body and so forth. The tensions may leave the body unresponsive and the organism unreceptive.

In sense awareness we take the same principle and use it to relax the body. We begin by rubbing out the tensions, by experiencing the breath release in a relaxed state, and, as the body begins to generalize the relaxed state, we begin to use the next principle: transfer.

Slowly as awareness and strength increase, we can begin to transfer the sensations we have had into more and more situations, more and more spaces and for longer and longer lengths of time. As Corrigan has said:

> The actor should attain a tension-free state which promotes a heightened inner awareness. At first this awareness is very diffused and rather non-specific, but as time goes on, as the student becomes more and more comfortable in the method, his sensory awareness is increased a thousandfold. [22]

GENERAL BODY AREAS: SPECIFIC TENSION AREAS

SKIN SENSATION
MUSCLE GROUPS

THE BACK RUB

We begin with two people, the "victim," who receives the back rub, and the one administering the massage.

Instructions to the person who administers the back rub:

1) rub/massage firmly but gently.
2) Slap vigorously, causing a stinging sensation.
3) Feel the person's structure -- the density of the flesh, the muscle

groups, the spine, the areas which carry the most tensions.

During some parts of the massage, close your eyes and let your hands "see."

Instructions to the "victim":

1) Enjoy and go with the sensations you will feel.
2) As the massage begins to reach the points where you carry tension, try to pinpoint where they are located. As they are "rubbed out" let them go.
3) Feel the rhythm of your breathing. Go with the rhythm.

Begin at the base of the neck and rub the muscles which extend up from the back of the neck down into the "muscle hanger" of the shoulders. Feel carefully as you go to locate tightness and knots. Rub them out gently. Take your time. Work in silence.

The shoulders usually carry too much weight, maintain too much support and generalize tensions which begin in the back and neck. Feel the strong muscles there and help relax them.

The neck generalizes tensions "wonderfully," too. The head tends to be an object of over-protection. The neck becomes stiff, full of tensions and inflexible. Move up and down the spinal column in the neck and rub out the tensions there. Hold the person's head in your strong hand and rub the occipital joint. This is the place where the skull and vertebrae join together. Bend your index finger and, using the second knuckle, rub the indentation that you will find there. Hold the head firmly and move it gently side to side. The victim should let his head become heavy and finally release its full weight into your hand.

Do not let the head go. Move slowly down the neck, find each of the seven vertebrae and rub them gently. The victim should begin to release the neck down, one vertebra at a time.

Let the head go gently. The victim should be standing with head stooped forward. Begin on the shoulders and back. Rub out the tensions, feel the structures. Put extra emphasis on the areas of tension and the lower back. When most of the tensions are released, then proceed to release the rest of the vertebrae down so that the person is bent at the waist. Again, take the person's head in your hands, do not let it go again until the person is fully released into the bent position.

Next begin to slap the back with both hands at the same time. Slap the entire surface especially the lower back. Move to the thighs and butt. Slap down each leg to the ankle. Move up the back again. Slap the arms and hands, than begin to tap the head gently. Let the fingers "rain" down all over the skull.

Massage the jaw muscle and the joint where it attaches to the skull. Find it by having the "victim" say the word "ouch." Rub this area gently.

Flop the arm to see if the person is relaxed there. Gently tap the head to see if it is still loose. Move away and let the person "enjoy" the sensations he feels in that position.

SENSE OF BODY ALIGNMENT

Begin to build the person up vertebra by vertebra. When he is standing erect again, begin to pull him "long." First, take one hand and place it at the back of the skull; then take the other hand and place it with thumb and index finger on the edge of the jaw and chin.

Lift the person up from the back of the skull. Stretch him out. Also, the hands may be placed with the palms over the jaw and the thumbs at the back of the ears. Try both ways and lift gently but with strength straight up. When the person is as long as possible, place your hands on the place where the shoulder and arm "cut an edge in space." Hold each shoulder firmly. Then, finger by finger, let them go. Let the victim stand silently and take in all the sensations that he can. Trade places and begin again.

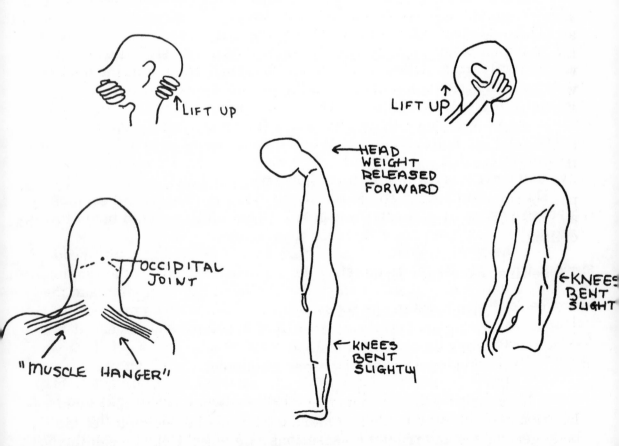

SENSE OF RHYTHM AND CAPACITY   NATURAL BREATHING

Next, lie on the floor and place your hand on your diaphragm area and the other on your abdomen. "Ride with whatever is there." Then when you feel like it, stand up again with as little effort as possible. Try to again sense the way you felt at the end of the backrub: the relaxation, the quiet breathing and the full length of the body in space.

STRETCH AND ALIGNMENT   NATURAL BREATHING

Next, shake out all over. Vibratory and swinging movements which encompass the major parts of the body are excellent ways to begin to relax. Shake out your hands, legs and begin to vibrate loosely all over. Collapse into the bent position again. As you fall, let any sound that you want fall out. "Ah," the "o" of "dome," "oo" of "who" are good loose sounds. Repeat the sound and let the sound fall out again.

SENSE OF ARTICULATORS AND   NATURAL BREATHING
RESONATORS

In the bent position begin to massage and "scrub" your face. The area of the sinuses, the nose, the jaw (massage the "ouch" point) should all be stimulated. As you scrub, let the sounds of "m" as in "map," the "ng" sound of "ringing" and "swinging" fall out and alternate the words "swinging" and "ringing" as you continue to scrub. Be sure that with every sound the air drops back into your lungs completely before you begin a new sound.

Again come up from the bent position, inhaling as you come and again collapse, this time with an exhalation. Repeat the collapse with the inhalation and exhalation.

Stretch toward the ceiling; stretch your arms as high as possible, pulling the whole body with them. Stretch out to the side, reach as far as possible. Again, stretch out to the other side. And once more to the ceiling.

These first exercises should:

1) stimulate deadened areas
2) bring about a general state of relaxation
3) work on specific tensions
4) develop a sense of proper alignment

If the actor works one hour a day five days a week, a state of relaxation should come more and more quickly as he begins to let his body generalize and transfer sensations. During the first week the back rub and similar sense relaxation exercises (group and individual) should be incorporated.

In about a week the "weaning away" from the back rub should begin as the actor is able, without assistance, to relax his own body. The production of sounds which open the throat and encompass the oral, nasal and head cavity should increase. Gradually, the articulation exercises are brought into the process.

These and more specific exercises should only begin and continue when and if the relaxation and connection with the natural breathing process is increased and trusted.

After the first week or so the pattern of workshop sessions becomes a microcosm of the entire method:

1) Segment for "warm-up"; stimulation; enlivening general areas of the body.
2) Segment for release of tensions/establishing proper alignment.
3) Work with developing strength and coordination of the articulators -- development of resonators.
4) Work with more and more specific problems centered on brief texts and scenes (i.e. simple maintenance of relaxation and keeping/trusting the natural breath connection).
5) Work with allowing the body to release into the impulses of the text without intellectual monitering.
6) Singing regularly under the guidance of a voice teacher in the Bel Canto method. This method of singing technique parallels the Iris Warren approach to vocal production. It is an essential complement to the actor training.

What follows is an outline of one two-hour workshop. This detailed description should serve to show how the method might work. Knowing the principles behind the Iris Warren method and the laws which govern the body, an actor should be able to devise his own progression of exercises as his individual demands are uncovered.

The warm-up and the sequence of movement which follow are used to explore 1) how the body should move; 2) proper sense of alignment; 3) a sense of stretch and strength throughout the joints; 4) development of strong but stretched muscles and 5) a development of agility and coordination. Dance can convey to the performer an understanding of movement in time and space. This understanding must occur to bring about an acceptance and use of change in rhythm and space relationships in the acting environment. The performer should understand physically that "up" can become as possible as "down." That is, the performer who can jump, hop, skip or leap with grace and rhythm can walk and run with ease, sureness and variety. The actor who has explored turning and stretching and moving backwards will find standing, walking or sitting in character on stage more exciting and dynamic.

The warm-up and sequence of exercises which follow are working toward the above ideas. All of the following exercises are accompanied by instructions in breathing and vocalization. On the left side of the page is an explanation of the physical movement and on the right is the explanation of the vocal and breathing exercises which occur simultaneously. The stick figures show the general body position and the arrows show the direction of movement of various body parts or the whole body.

The warm-up should be looked upon as a way of tuning the body for the most sensitive and rewarding exploration possible. The actor should get out of his ordinary pedestrian rhythm and stimulate his breathing and heart rate. The warming up of specific muscle groups is necessary so his body can approach activity "lubricated" and breathing fully. One must be careful never to hold the breath in any of the following exercises. Breathing should be as relaxed and full as possible.

WARM-UP

Body Movement	Voice Movement
(1) Begin with a simple walk in a straight line. Walk with the heels striking the ground first and easily. Focus on the direction you are walking. Go there with assurance.	Start with an easy humming. The sounds "oo" as in "fool" or "ah" as in "father." Elongate the sound. Make it move in the direction you you are going. Feel the sound is ahead of you. Do not force the humming. Imagine you have a golf ball in your mouth.

Do the walk-humming the full length of the room.
Return to where you started with the same walk-hum.

(2) At the end of each walk collapse from the hips and let the head and arms become relaxed and heavy. Do not hold the head or shoulders. Swing from the waist gently to the left and right. Let the head and arms move with the swinging torso.	Exhale as you collapse. Exhale completely.

Let the air come in fully and gently. Feel what happens in your lower back and abdominals as you exhale and inhale.
As you swing begin to sound the "m" and "ah" of "ma." Work it on |
| Roll through the spine from the tail bone to the top of the neck. Feel the full roll of the spine. | your lips and continue to feel the image of a golf ball in your mouth. |
| Reach the arms above the head without raising the shoulders and let the stretching take you | As you begin to reach let your head fall back and cease vocalizing. |

Body Movement	Voice Movement

easily to half toe. Reach through the hip joint and let the torso continue stretching-reaching from each hip. Stretch as long as possible. Then slowly come to balanced alignment. Feel that the chest and hips are resting over one another and the head rests easily on top of them. Feel the length of the torso.

As you come to balanced alignment let all the air out. Full exhalation. Then let the air flood easily in. As you feel the stretch in the torso feel what is happening in your lower back and abdominals as you inhale.

(3)   Repeat (1) and (2) in varied tempos. Begin slowing and progress to a rapid walk -- not a run. Do not stiffen the legs.
Relax the knee and foot.

(4)   Repeat (1) and (2), this time walking with toes touching the
floor first. Work on stretching through the knee, ankle
and toes. Do not lock the knees. Again walk at varied tempos, this time progressing to a run. Work through the
knees. Work for stretch and relaxation in the torso and
flexibility in the knees and feet.

(5) Begin a random walk. (Walk in any direction, changing direction as often as you feel necessary.) As you walk begin to float in space. Feel that your body is floating. Float in one direction and then let the floating take you in another direction. Cease to plan your direction in space. Float, fall and turn.

Use vowel sounds as you begin to float. After making initially easy open sounds allow the voice to make whatever sound it wants to. As you walk-float feel your breath falling in and out. Monitor what is happen-ing; do not interfere. For a time walk-float with your breathing rhy-thm. Pause, stopping movement and sound, between the periods of exhala-tion and inhalation. Be careful not to hold your breath at any time.

(6) At some point in floating begin to stretch and expand your body in as many directions as possi-ble. Stretch various body parts as long as they will go. Grow-stretch slowing in the arms,neck legs, shoulders, torso and feet. Grow-stretch at different speeds. Stretch out of your joints. Feel the impulse to lengthen coming

Move your head, face, tongue and lips as if they were operating on ball bearings. As you move begin to use the sound of "oo" as in "food." As you move into the center of your body make "oo" sounds and as you stretch into space make "ah" sounds.

Begin to stretch your lips, tongue, face and neck in as many ways as

Body Movement	Voice Movement

from the center of those joints. Grow the extra inch through all the joints. Stretch until you are exhausted. Work standing and lying on the floor. Stretch until you must be quiet. Then slowly come to standing in a centered and balanced alignment.

possible. Stretch them as far as possible. Alternate the stretching with limp relaxation of the lips and tongue. Let the tongue hang on the lips heavily and make a loose "fa-fa-fa" as in "father" sound. Feel the jaw hanging heavily. At points where the body is stretched to its longest, isolate and relax the face, neck, tongue and lips. Blow air out the lips loosely.
As you end the section stop vocalizing and monitor the movement and progress of your breathing. Just feel what is there; do not interfere.

(7) When you feel the center begin to glide randomly, bend your knees and glide as smoothly as you can. Begin to feel you are flying. Fly vigorously, soar, turn, glide and float. Glide slowly. Run and glide.

Use the "o" of "dome" and the "fv" sound on your lips. Monitor tension in your neck and throat. Fill your body with your own vibrations. Feel the sounds in your head, neck, chest, knees and hands. Feel the tensions escaping with the sounds.

(8) Move as though your body were filled with ball bearings. Let everything rotate inside and out.

Repeat Voice section (6).

(9) Stand in Modern Dance First Position. Heels touching and the toes comfortably apart. Come to a balanced alignment. Keeping your feet in place, begin to sway slowly in all directions.

Repeat Voice section (7). Roll your neck and head as you sway in easy circles.

(10) Standing in first position, lean forward gently as far as possible. Do not move your feet. Lean gently backward. Repeat leaning forward and backward. Begin to bounce easily, lifting the heels slightly. Tap the floor gently with your heels. Keep the knees and ankles flexible and relaxed. Bounce faster until it becomes an easy vibration throughout the entire body.

Continue Voice section (9).

Body Movement	Voice Movement

Walk, continue the vibration
through the whole body. Shake
the arms and shoulders vigorously.

After moving several times a-
round the room vibrating, collapse from the hip. Hang gently
and roll up the spine. Come to
a balanced alignment.

Sigh and yawn. Then monitor what is
there. Feel the movement of your
breathing. Let sound fall out randomly on your exhalations. Do not interfere with the rhythm.

Warm-up and movement sequence
follow one another immediately.

MOVEMENT SEQUENCE

All dance combinations or patterns of movement work upon the
performer in a multidimensional way. A strong pattern will develop
the performer's sense of how the body can and should move. The dance
sequence will make the performer more aware of specific parts of his
body; how these work in isolation and how they work together. A com-
prehensive movement sequence will provide a strong sense of the dynamics of movement both rhythmically and spatially. Mary Wigman
once defined dance as "movement in time and space." The principles
of movement and elements of dance composition are inherent in every
play and in every character's physical development.

It is important that the actor develop this sense of movement; the
shape of his body in space and the space and rhythmic factors of movement. The movement sequence which follows works with these factors
as did the warm-up which precedes it. If the actor does not understand
or sense his own body spatially and rhythmically, how can he knowledge-
ably develop a character's body shape and use space and rhythm for the
character in a play?

This sequence is designed to explore some anatomical limits, develop awareness of muscles and how they function, and to redistribute
specific muscle strengths with the articulation and isolation of the joints.
The specific muscle strengths worked upon here will improve the res-
piration process, can improve alignment and bring the actor ease and
economy of movement.

This particular sequence deals with abdominal strengths. It works
to stretch and contract the major muscle groups of the back and abdomen. Begin the sequence with a balanced alignment and a deep inhalation.

Body Movement	Voice Movement
1) From first position stretch slowly upward in four counts. Do not raise the shoulders. Stretch through the torso, hips, ankles and feet. Come to a fully stretched foot, balanced on your toes. Press the abdominals in and keep the rib cage down. The lower back should be as straight as possible.	Blow your air out gently as if you were blowing the fuzz off a dandelion. A whole field of dandelions. Monitor tensions in the neck and throat. Let them blow out gently.
	When you have let all the air blow out, let the air fall in again easily and as deeply as possible. Sense if you are blocking the inhalation.
2) Contract slowly in four counts. The head down and face coming to the knees. Become as tight a ball as possible. Feet are flat on the floor. Fold arms around legs and try not to sit down, but keep the hips down and in.	As you sink down let your air fall out. Use the "o" of "dome" and the "ah" of "mama." Feel the vibrations throughout your entire body. Let the air come in again and feel in the tight contraction how the air fills your body.
3) Repeat (1).	Repeat (1).
4) Repeat (2).	Repeat (2). Blow all the air out through relaxed lips (the gentle raspberries!).
5) Repeat (1) in four counts.	As you stretch, feel relaxation in the chest and shoulders. Let the air fall in -- flood in! Do not force the inhalation.

6) Fall forward in one count. On the second count let your right leg slide out and catch you. Fall over the thigh. Let your back foot turn over. Collapse through the head and neck and shoulders. Let the whole torso relax.	As you fall forward let the air fall out too. Let whatever sound happens fall out with the breath.
7) Repeat (5). Make the effort to pull the hips under as you bring your left leg through to standing.	Repeat (5).
8) Repeat (6).	Repeat (6).

Body Movement	Voice Movement

(9) Repeat (7).

Repeat (7).

(10) Transfer your weight to your right. Let the left leg bend. Stretch toward the right.

Make an elongated "who" sound at a very high pitch. Men use falsetto. Let the sound float out through your fingers.

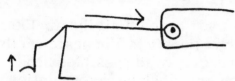

Press your abdominals inward. Straighten your lower back. Look forward with the head between the arms. Feel the stretch through the torso and hips, not through the shoulders.

(11) Hold this position for two counts; grow through the stretch.

Continue to sound (10) until all the air is out.

(12) Come to a wide second position -- your legs turned out from the hips and the knees over the feet equally.

Let the air come in -- flood in! Do not stop or control the flow.

(13)-(17) Repeat (9) through (12).

Repeat (9) through (12).

(18) Arabesque. Lift the left leg behind you and extend the standing leg fully. Reach out and upward through the chest and arms in four counts.

Full inhalation.

(19) Hold stretching for four counts.

Air goes through the lips on exhalation -- "fa-fa-fa" as in "father." Spray paint a pastel color on the space in front of you.

REMAIN STRETCHED

BEND STANDING LEG

Body Movement	Voice Movement
(20) Bend the standing leg. Remain fully extended as the leg bends down in eight counts.	Gasping inhalation in two counts. Lap like a cat, the tongue loose in your mouth. Exhalation in six counts.
(21) Get as close to the ground as you can.	

(22) Turn over toward the left leg and stretch out full on your back. Hold this position for an uncounted inhalation.	Let the air fall in. Feel you have been filled up from the bottoms of your feet to the tips of your fingers.

(23) Relax the entire body. Let everything go.	Let the air fall out. Monitor your exhalation and focus on the movement and sensation of your breathing.
(24)	Make a complete inhalation.
(25) Reach hands to the toes, the torso and legs reaching and extending as far as possible in four counts. Back and legs must be straight and extended.	Exhale with an easy open sound falling out.

V

(26) Come to (22) in four counts.	Repeat (22).
(27) Roll over on to your stomach. Repeat (23) trying to reach the hands to the toes. Torso and legs straight and extended.	Exhalation with tongue relaxed on lower lip. Let air vibrate tongue. Strong vigorous raspberries!
(28)-(33) Repeat (22) through (27)	Repeat (22) through (27).

Body Movement	Voice Movement

(34) Roll over on your back. Cross left leg over right thigh as close to the hip as possible.

Inhalation.

(35) Contract abdominals. Sit up as you pull your right leg under you.

Exhalation with easy open sounds.

(36) Step on to left foot and arabesque. Extend your standing leg, right leg stretched behind.

Inhalation.

(37) Swing right leg through and make a half turn. Come to position #1. Focus is up toward the ceiling.

Exhalation.

(38) Lower heels to the floor in four counts and bring the arms slowly down. Come to a balanced alignment.

Monitor your breathing. Do not interfere. Let yourself be breathed.

Explanation of movement sequences (1) through (9):

Movements (1) through (9) deal with the idea of opening and closing. The actor should sense what feelings he associates with opening and closing. How does he feel toward these two actions? Movement through these sections should begin very slowly. Emphasis is placed on executing the movements correctly.

Explanation of movement sequences (9) through (38):

Sequences (9) through (38) deal primarily with shape and line. Emphasis here should be placed on sensations of stretching through the joints. Also attention should be paid to the tactile and kinesthetic senses in relation to how the body feels in space. When is it emphasizing line and when shape and weight? Again, these sections are performed slowly at first. Each actor may use his own images related to the body moving in space.

Repeat all the sequences on the opposite side of the body. This time emphasize ease and flow. The actor should begin to develop a sense of each movement flowing into the next. Speed up the counting slightly.

Repeat all of the sequences on both sides. This time establish, with musical accompaniment, a formal rhythm. Allow the body to move with the rhythms and execute the movement in relationship to their rhythmic flow. How do different rhythms change the dynamics of the entire sequence?

The fourth time the actor should work in a small group. The problem is to divide the sequence into simple sections. Then work to change the qualities of movement: percussive, sustained, abrupt, collapsing and swinging. Create a simple composition using parts of the sequence and qualities of movement or rhythms. Each group should develop an improvisation, putting parts of the sequence together with various rhythms.

PROBLEM SOLVING

Develop a simple repeatable pattern of movement with a shape and sound from a character in a play. Any period or genre. Example: Frankie from Member of the Wedding; Puck from A Midsummer Night's Dream; Blanche from A Streetcar Named Desire; or John Proctor from The Crucible. Design a movement and sound composition which moves across the room. When the movement and sound composition is completed, choose a key passage spoken by the character you have chosen. The passage may be a soliloquy or long speech spoken to another character, about 20 lines. Work with the basic spatial elements of holes, doors, windows and boxes. Develop a new composition using the words and the mimed spaces. How does the language affect the spaces? What do the character's feelings do to the composition? How would the character use these spaces? Are these spaces to be literal holes, windows, boxes or doors? Are the spaces psychological rather than literal? The actor must deal in some way with both kinds of space and make it clear which is literal and which abstract. The words and the spaces must also include the age, sex and cultural traits of the character.

CONCLUSION

The actor must come to understand that a play can be a repeatable and precise sequence of movements. These sequences (Stanislavsky called them beats; dancers might term them phrases) make up the visual expression of the character and the play as a conceptual whole. The play if performed without words should be an expressive piece of choreography which could stand alone as a composition. Through the careful integration of the Iris Warren principles and modern dance techniques, the actor can develop a sense of sequence and composition, sensory awareness of his body structure and how it moves, and an understanding of his perceptions and how they feed the creative process of the performer. The actor should be guided through the rehearsal and performance by the principles which govern the physical structure of the body and our perceptions. An intellectual understanding does not provide the actor with tools. He must work regularly with the organic unity of voice and body -- eliminating the separation in training.

Modern dance techniques provide the actor with a responsiveness to all the perceptual input of his body. The dance can create for the actor a body sensitive to shape, line, direction and rhythms. Through dance training the actor can develop a sense of varied qualities of movement and the coordination to use them creatively. Modern dance technique and the Iris Warren method of voice production give the actor the opportunity, as Mary Corrigan stated:

> to learn to react immediately and organically to signals (feelings) which are generated below the conscious level of his brain. It is absolutely essential that the actor no longer "think" about what he is doing .... This method seeks a spontaneously organic response to the text from the whole person; it seeks an immediate and intuitive response which is not hampered by intellectualizing. "[23]

NOTES

1. John M. Wilson, Lecture on Dance Philosophy, University of Utah, January 11, 1971.

2. Suzanne K. Langer, Feeling and Form, Scribners, 1953. p. 307.

3. Viola Spolin, Improvisation for the Theatre, Northwestern University Press, 1963. p. 15.

4. Spolin. p. 16.

5. Jerzy Grotowski, Towards a Poor Theatre, Simon and Schuster, 1969. p. 208.

6. Mary K. Corrigan, Radio Interview, KUER, University of Utah, Salt Lake City, August 29, 1967.

7. Fritz Perls, Gestalt Therapy Verbatim, Real People Press, 1969. p. 11.

8. Wolfgang von Buddenbrock, The Senses, University of Michigan Press, 1958. p. 12.

9. Rudolph Arneim, Art and Visual Perception, University of California, 1954. p. vi.

10. Perls. p. 12.

11. Perls. p. 13.

12. Margeret H' Doubler, Dance, A Creative Art Experience, University of Wisconsin Press, 1957. p. 149.

13. H' Doubler. p. 149.

14. Corrigan, KUER Interview.

15. Corrigan, KUER Interview.

16. Arnheim, p. vii.

17. H' Doubler. p. 149.

18. Grotowski. p. 250.

19. Grotowski. p. 254.

20. Stanley Burnshaw, The Seamless Web, Braziller, 1970. p. 186.

21. Arnheim. p. 1.

22. Corrigan. KUER Interview.

23. Corrigan. KUER Interview.

NOTES ON ORGANIC TRAINING

DUNCAN ROSS

The term "organic" is often used indiscriminately. It is invoked to convey a vague feeling of "totality" of an ad hoc approach, or letting it "all just happen. "

Let's be specific. "Organism" is the category of events in which the internal relations of functions continuously change in order to maintain the continuance of the entity which they constitute. (A. N. Whitehead pointed out that this is now how we view an atom so that "organism" no longer applies exclusively to living entities.)

What this model, therefore, involves can be regarded from two points of view: (1) the constant spontaneous changing of the balance of function within the organism, and (2) that these are goal oriented.

For our purposes in actor training, we may take these two aspects as fundamental principles. Taking (2) first -- all training exercises must be structured as problem-solving situations, with a goal beyond the actual "how" of doing something.

(1) is probably the most interesting approach. In practical terms it entails turning the attention of the student on to some aspect of his behavior which is not the thing you are trying to develop but which will, through the spontaneous adjustments of the organism, modify that behavior which the teacher wants to get at. Thus a lack of relaxation which shows itself as stiffness when the student is standing still can be helped by externalizing an inner monologue -- through the actual lines of the actor. Or, a particular vocal quality can be assisted by asking the actor to dance the whole scene in a tempo that will lead him towards the vocal expression.

In the development of imagery the same principle can be used. Do not ask the student to concentrate on the particular mode of imagery you want developed; divert his attention to another mode related to the given circumstances. Thus, if tactile manipulation is the problem, ask the student to vocally describe the sensations of touch, weight, heat, etc., or even divert his attention to imagining the smells or sounds that might be present. Most failures of the imagination are related to anxiety to achieve. Diversion of attention from the area of anxiety nearly always opens the channels of the imagination.

This diversion of attention from the central problem begins to help the student to understand that "concentrating on concentrating" is a destructive approach. Imagining must be handled lightly and should be something that occupies the periphery of awareness. Central attention should be on the goal of the scene -- everything else should be "put in the periphery."

I have observed that many actors develop vocal problems when anxiety obtrudes. Worry about "projection" is one of the most destructive concerns for the actor.

Place the actors involved in a scene throughout the theatre -- on the stage, around the auditorium, in the balcony, etc. Tell them to play the scene roving around the theatre. It quickly becomes obvious that they can be heard throughout the house. From this they get a sense of imagining in the whole volume of the theatre without strain -- there is nobody with normal vocal organs who cannot carry on a conversation with somebody at the back of the house. When the students return to the stage, they must keep that awareness of speaking through the whole volume of the house while they are only a few feet from their acting partner. Several sessions of playing the scene in the whole theatre may be necessary to establish this awareness in the "periphery."

On the other hand many actors -- including myself -- are capable of making all sorts of sounds which on first hearing should impair their vocal organs. I have only lost my voice once in the theatre, during a production directed by Michel St. Denis. (Olivier records the same fact -- the only place where our abilities might be said to coincide!) This was because St. Denis kept insisting on a certain sound. But the most unusual and striking sounds can be produced if the attention of the actor stays away from the voice. Immersion in the physical imagery of the role and the use of movement simultaneously with sound produces spontaneous colors impossible to produce when thinking about the voice.

The kinesthetic aspect of meaning is now well established in linguistics. By using the large voluntary muscle groups of the hands and arms to play out the kinesthetic aspect of words, greater meaning and wider ranges of tone color are produced spontaneously.

These "movement feelings" of the words can be progressively developed -- from the hands and arms to the pelvis. The fullness of tone and the corresponding spontaneous use of diaphragm can be quite remarkable. Later these actual movements may be reduced to "shadow" movements -- almost images of the sense of the larger movements.

This kinesthetic approach organizes the words into phrases of meaning spontaneously -- "actions" which are then played with objectives on another person.

An "objective," in my jargon, is an attempt to change the emotional state of the person to whom you are playing the objective.

Choice of "objective" is considered by imagining in one's own muscles what response the action should achieve in the partner if the action were to be successful. "How do you want him to react? Show me." "O.K.

now keep the image of what you have just shown and try to get it from your partner."

The idea of resonators is, of course, physiologically largely "eye wash," but to imagine the voice is reverberating in various parts of the body can produce interesting modifications of the pharynx. This can sometimes be helped by taking two students who have been asked to imagine their voices are coming out of their backs. (Gibberish sounds should be used -- perhaps developed from movements). If the two students then place their backs against each other and then converse -- develop objectives -- with the vibrations they feel from one another, interesting vocal qualities occur. Of course, any part of the body can be used.

The technique of limiting the physical means of communicating often provides a strong organizing stimulus. Placing a screen between two actors and forbidding either to answer their cues until the other actor's speech makes them want to respond has possibilities on occasion. The use of masks is a technique well developed by LeCog for bodily discipline, but it can also be a valuable stimulus to vocal expression. Performing difficult physical tasks with objects also often organizes the voice -- and takes the self-conscious attention away from sound.

But in all these techniques, great care must be taken to avoid "acting at" the partner. Always the central concern is to get an emotional response from the other actor. This is "acting with" your colleague. Much of the "experimental theatre" acting one sees is ultimately a sham since it is really nothing more than highly sophisticated "mugging."

PATTERNS OF LIFE; PATTERNS OF ART

SALLY R. SOMMER

     To say that art and life reflect each other, that performance activity and everyday activity are interrelated, is to state the obvious. And yet, it is "obvious" only in the most intuitive sense, because the exact nature of that relationship has been unclear. Unfortunately for performing arts, investigations about this relationship have been carried out almost exclusively by philosophers and theoreticians. And even more unfortunate is the fact that the most highly visible of these investigators has been the critic, and that the "analytic" tool has been so inexact: critical aesthetics are metaphysical, philosophical and theoretical. The connections critics have made between performance and life are speculative, saturated by opinion and restricted by the particular perceptual narrowness of their time. This does not mean that aesthetics have been entirely useless and inelegant. But it does mean, as any researcher can tell, that the records of performances, the data necessary for any comparative study with society, are either short, snappy and personal (critic/reviewer), or long, convoluted and turgid (philosopher/aesthetician). At any rate, too little has been descriptive of the events. "Data" have been the plays, and comparative studies have been literary, not to be confused with theater which is a performing, humanly interactional art. The problem is really two-fold: if one abstract system (aesthetics) is used to describe another abstract system (art), it is bound to be fuzzy; and basically, these two systems most often refer only to each other, making it an intramural contest.

     In seeking to define art, definitions get turned into rules and regulations, standards by which to judge what is "good" and what is "bad" art. Arbitrary boundaries and divisions are created, effectively compartmentalizing one art form after another. This hierarchical grid separates what kinds of movements are "dance," what kinds of sounds are "music" and what kinds of activities are theatre." It makes it so easy to dismiss any work that doesn't fit. We can define and keep apart "popular entertainment" from the "artistic," and we can speak comfortably of "legitimate" and "illegitimate" theatre. Aesthetic theory always lags behind the actuality of performing. In avant-garde and experimental forms, the work is most often seen long before it is fortified by critical/theoretical acceptance. The forward thrust of the avant-garde appears to create a vacuum between form and theory as it obliterates established definitions.

Interestingly enough, this gap also exists in science -- between observed phenomena and theory. But the evidence is not ignored in as cavalier a fashion in this discipline as the evidence of "bad" performance is ignored by critics. "Perception and value are inseparably fused, but conscious and intentional value judgments can be lessened."[1] The methodology of science tries very hard to be objective, and resultant data must be verifiable and checkable by consensus. The "art" of designing the good scientific study is to reduce to a minimum the bias and unreliability of the perceiver, to seek the ultimate objective description.

The way science goes about establishing links between phenonema and theory could be useful and transferable into investigations about performance. The connections between science and art are many: both are involved in expanding our awareness and offering us new perceptions about experience. Not infrequently scientists and artists work on the same problems. Cubism demonstrated certain principles of prismatic refraction; pointillism is a visual analogue of the molecular theory of light. Even more essential are performances whose recapitulations of myth, dream, psychology and constellations of almost precognitive images long foreshadowed scientific "discoveries" of such mental patterns.

John Cage has said that value judgments are destructive to our business, which is curiosity and awareness. Michael Kirby stated that most criticism as it is now practiced is immoral, primitive and arrogant. Richard Schechner says that critics have not learned from the "advances in fields contiguous to performance -- such as the social sciences -- that have begun to develop methodologies for dealing with 'life' situations.... There is a methodology of criticism that can be developed on the basis of sociologic models."[2]

Recently, scientific methods have been used to study communication systems, both verbal and nonverbal. Communications systems are seen as part of behavior -- which is both an expression of, and a regulation of, the social structures and adaptive patterns of a culture. This means that performance behavior and everyday behavior make up a continuum, do not represent different spheres of behavior, but are simply two expressions of the same continuum, drawing material from the same experiential pool. This method offers a way of looking at the processes of performing and nonperforming as shared behavior. (It levels those distinctions of "natural vs unnatural," "real vs unreal" set up in aesthetics about performance.)

An understanding of art, of man's nature, and of his culture can be broadened, deepened, and quickened by uncovering the associations, dependencies, the derivations which unite the various aspects of man's emergence and invention. [3]

A method of structural analysis applied to performance is being done by a group of anthropologists and dance analysts. The project "Choreometrics -- or the study of dance and movement style as a measure of society"[4] is directed by Alan Lomax and sponsored by Columbia University, Department of Anthropology, Bureau of Applied Social Research. The project began in 1968 with the initial collaboration of anthropologists and dance analysts Irmgard Bartenieff and Forrestine Paulay; Choreometrics grew out of the previous Cantometrics Project (the study of song style as a measure of society) set up in 1961 by Lomax and Dr. Conrad Arensberg and musicologist Victor Grauer.

The underlying idea in both these studies is that art (expressive patterns) reflect life (culture patterns); but there is more than mere reflection, there is a dynamic effect produced on the society from the art. Although the culture determines the original components (behavior) used by the artist, the thing created (performed dance and song) "have a status and continuity of their own apart from the cultural realities from which they stem and for which they stand. This concept cannot be too much emphasized since it rescues the reasonable man from the trap of cultural determinism."[5] In other words, there is a reciprocity between art and society and that each shapes the other. "The dance, then, seen in this light, is a reinforcement of human adaptive patterns and can thus be used as an index of social evolution."[6]

The science of Choreometrics, as Lomax says, is still in a "fledgling" state. Basically, it is still at the stage of observation and the recordings of those observations. But the logical and fundamental assumption is that through description, classification and codification -- rather than interpretation and empathy -- a theory can be developed which could explain something about art's connection with the rest of culture.

Choreometrics attempts by applying methods of structural analysis to uncover what interrelations exist between society and the performed arts. And they do this by looking at behavior. By describing and scoring everyday activity and dance activity in the same descriptive terms, they hope to discover what movements are essential to each set of activities, and if those essential movements are the same. These observations are rated, and on the basis of statistical evidence the researchers will be able to do an internal

37

comparison within a single culture between dance and workaday behavior, and will be able to do a cross-cultural comparison to answer how dance styles vary from culture to culture, what these differences are, and, finally, what they signify.

It is important to understand that Choreometrics does not describe step-by-step movement, but describes how a people move, the style of movement. As stated by Lomax in Choreometrics and Ethnographic Filmmaking, this broader level of description deals with how the body is handled in terms of "a) body parts most frequently articulated, b) shape of the movement path and of transitions, c) body attitude and active stance [postural modes], d) patterns that link body and limb, e) dynamic qualities."[7] This last is probably one of the most crucial determinants in style -- an idea about movement postulated originally by Rudolph von Laban in his Effort/Shape theory. It has to do with how people use their energy, the exertion they use in the approach to tasks, the ebb and flow of energy.

One of the important things to remember is that although this system is purposely broad in its description, it does not negate the rich and varied expression of idiosyncratic personal movement. It simply describes a level of movement more fundamental and basic -- a cultural style. Lomax sees this as "a dynamic that is postulated to shape all types of communications within any culture, area or tradition."[8] He refers to this as a "supportive base line" of movement, or a "movement signature;" individually particular movement will then grade away from this basic movement signature, which acts more as a statement of cultural affiliation. The concept of style operates on the social level. "This style seems to serve two main functions for all individuals: 1) Identification: it identifies the individual as a member of his culture who understands and is in tune with its communication systems. 2) Synchrony: it forms and molds together the dynamic quality which make it possible for the members of a culture to act together in dance, work, movement, love-making, speech -- in fact in all their interactions."[9]

On a more general level, Choreometrics describes those elements which serve to unite the group and make it a whole, rather than a collection of individual activities. This includes such things as the rhythmic pattern, moving the same limbs, moving in the same direction, sharing a focus, maintaining the same distance from each other. Also included are the sex of the participants, whether they perform together or separately, or as separate components within a group, act in paired relationships, how many people participate and what their relationships are ie., led or leaderless.

Quite obviously, using the parameters of how the body is handled and how the group unites, one can see how these descriptions could work for performance or for everyday work. "Any human event, scenes of work, ritual, everyday life, can be analyzed in Choreometric terms."[10] This was one of the most basic problems for the researchers to solve -- how to arrive at that level of movement which was common, and how to then describe it in understandable terms so it could then be applied cross-culturally. The cross-cultural nature of the study is important, because no general statement about the nature of art could be made unless more than one culture is studied -- and unless more than one expressive system is used; this is why Cantometrics lead to Choreometrics, and one would assume that there will be yet another study of another art form in the future. Lomax and his group's primary goal was "to produce a rating system for looking at human behavior which would one day be understandable to anyone who wanted to use it.... The system was to rest upon the main qualitative differences in aspects of behavior which every human being has to learn from his parents in order to exhibit cultural affiliation."[11] Further detailed studies show that spatial relations, timing, in fact all behaviors that govern interaction are learned at a very early age, in exchanges of "real behavior" between mother and child. (See an interview with Daniel Stern, TDR (T-59).)

Film was to provide the raw data for the Choreometric study. Film can permanently record a transitory performing art, it can be endlessly repeated and it can be stored for future reference. Filmed records too have their perceptual biases, depending on who and how they were shot, but a filmed record can be more reliable and objective than written description. For many years, filmed documentaries of the life activities of various cultures have been collected by anthropologists. "The total corpus of film of human beings shot and stored since the invention of the movie camera is the richest data bank of human behavior we have."[12] In Toward an Ethnographic Film Archive Lomax sensibly states in rebuttal to those who would not use what film exists because of its potential bias: "...since motion pictures of human behavior are layer cakes of structured communication patterns, there is ethnographic data of some sort in all documentary footage (which hasn't been chopped absolutely to pieces), if not at the fine-grained level, then at a grosser one. This is not to say that we should not have data standards and that they should not improve, but rather that our fledgling science should learn to use what is already in the record."[13]

The Choreometric coding procedures are extremely detailed, although the methods are intentionally coarse. It is a testament to the rigor of the scientific and social scientific methodology that "broad" descriptions are, in fact, so fine-grained. (I would refer anyone interested to read Lomax's book Folk Song Style and Culture, chapters on Choreometrics, co-authored by Lomax, Irmgard Bartenieff and Forrestine Paulay, pp. 222-73.)

Choreometrics has studied hundreds of small, homogeneous societies where there has been little melting-pot mixing of cultural patterns. As the science develops, it will be able to turn its attention to the more complicated groups (such as the United States) which exhibit complex and rich cultural mixes.

What the researchers have discovered is that there is in fact a very tight correlation between dance activity and kinds of work important in a culture. "The movement style in dance is a crystallization of the most frequent and crucial patterns of everyday activity."[14] These correlations are significant enough to support the idea that the performed art of any society is really a sensitive indicator of that society, and in fact offers an immediate "model" of that culture. "Choreometrics affirms the existence of a very few large and very old style traditions: 1) the primitive Pacific, 2) black Africa with Melanesia and Polynesia, 3) high culture Eurasia and 4) Europe....also an Arctic style tradition that links northern Europe across Siberia to aboriginal North America."[15] Obviously these style traditions seem to follow the paths of the great human migrations which implies that there are "communication styles which are extremely stable across time and whose life spans extend for hundreds, perhaps thousands of years."[16]

At this point, it might be interesting to have some examples of how the Choreometric correlations work: (The following descriptions are taken from a much longer, detailed passage in Folk Song Style and Culture, pp. 336-7. It is only one of many such descriptions of many different cultures.) The dance of the Netsilik Eskimo hunters takes place in the large communal igloo. The women sit, grouped, and chant as the dancer (the male, the hunter), each in succession, executes a solo performance of drumming, singing and dancing. The manner in which the women are present for the dancing parallels a characteristic structure in the culture. The women's role in this society "who play a part in the productive operation equal to that of the men" is to wait at the camp for the hunter, "receive the game, and process it into edible food and clothing." They "portray this role exactly in the scene described, by singing a song in the 'chewing' rhythm they use all day as they soften the skins brought by their men." This is a striking similarity in social and performing structures.

> One after another, the greatest hunters stand up before the group, a large flat drum covered with sealskin in the left hand, a short, clublike drumstick in the other...holding the wide stance used by these Eskimos when they walk through ice and snow or stand in the icy water fishing.

The dancer uses the body as a strong, supportive base for the movements of the arms. The feet are placed apart, wide based; the knees bend slightly as the right arm chops downward and straighten as the arm is raised for the upstroke; all the while the left arm is steadily rotated as it helps in the twisting motion of the drum as it turns from side to side.

> Each stroke of the short drumstick goes diagonally down and across to hit the lower edge of the drum and turn the drumhead. On the backstroke it strikes the other edge, reversing the motion which is then carried through by a twist of the left forearm.... A good dancer must stand and drum in this fashion for a long time without failing in the rhythm or losing his drive.

The endurance of the dancer replicates one of the necessary qualities for the Eskimo hunter who must stand for hours, waiting in stillness for the seal to come to the air hole, and when it comes to thrust the harpoon "diagonally across the chest with the full force of the compact and solidly held trunk behind it."

> The salmon-fisher stands hip-deep in the clear waters of the weir, thrusting his spear down and across, lifting the speared fish clear of the water, twisting it off the barb and threading it on the cord at his waist in a series of swift, strong, straight, angular movements tied together by powerful rotations of the forearm.

These descriptions demonstrate quite clearly how dance is a formalized transformation of everyday activity, a reflection of those behaviors and values so necessary for maintenance of the society. These correlations may perhaps seem simple and one could assume that they would be easily observable. That is true, and such observations indeed gave rise to the working hypothesis of Choreometrics. But any hypothesis must be substantiated by data, and a method must be found by which to extract and then analyze the information. "It is so commonplace to observe that stance, gesture, fashion of moving and above all, dancing vary from culture to culture and have very much to say about the nature of a people. But only recently have new techniques been developed to enable the observer to specify exactly what these differences are and what they signify." (Italics mine.)[17] This is the first time that a systematic study has been done and rigorous scientific investigations have been applied in the gathering of evidence in this area. And there is something quite marvelous about the fact that the search for these proofs has brought together two disciplines which have traditionally been so far apart.

Margaret Mead and Gregory Bateson pioneered the use of film and photographic studies as an information source in their analysis of the relationship between Balinese character and dance to child-rearing practices, The Balinese Character, 1942. This study acted as a catalyst in bringing together linguists and researchers in body communication, and infused energetic interest into the fields of non-verbal communication studies. From these studies, a new methodology for looking at the visible stream of behavioral activity developed, the "kinesic" analysis of movement.

Very simply, this kinesic analysis studies frame by frame, at shutter speeds ranging from 1/24 to 1/40 per second, film of human interaction. Daniel Stern, another kinesic researcher, has described its purpose: "take the event out of its usual time frame -- you see it differently and freshly. (...) the issue isn't how to get smaller and smaller units but how to change the time scale of the investigator's viewing of the units so that he can re-put together the pattern of events and get some notion of their structure."[18]

Dr. Ray Birdwhistell, pioneer and leader in the field of kinesics, discovered at this slowed rate a level of body movement not noticeable at normal rates. This movement formed its own "kinesic" body language, as formal and complex as verbal communication; human beings are constantly immersed in this kinesic stream of movement which is culturally learned and passed on generationally from parent to child. They are an essential part of "multi-commu-nication channels" which are "interdependently merged." The con-joining of the multi-channels generates meaning and context, and those meanings and contexts vary from culture to culture. Bird-whistell also found "assemblages of movement" so crucial to "organ-ized social interaction" that they in fact weld it together. He calls them "motion qualities" and they function at the level of identification; although what these movements are differ from culture to culture, a constellation of these movements must be present in order to forge a group into one of social membership. These movements act as the base and cement for interactional exchanges.

William Condon discovered another principle of this kinesic movement -- synchrony. These movements do not operate in terms of action/reaction, but at the level of simultaneity. Comparing the micro-phonetic record with micro-kinetic activity observable on film, he found that a listener, in order to understand, must move in synchronous harmony with the speaker; and that the speaker, in turn, moves in rhythm with his phonation. Understanding is being "in tune" with the phonation, and all within earshot are involved in a synchronous dance with all other members of the group.

Birdwhistell referred to those "motion qualities" necessary for organized social interaction as "cross-referencing identification behaviors." This observation about certain kinds of movements would later provide the base for Lomax's conception of style, and would be fundamental in determining Choreometric parameters: "...it reaches out to another level, to the level of identification where signals, constantly flowing in the kinesic stream, characterize all present in terms of age, sex, occupation and most especially, cul-tural affiliation. Birdwhistell shows that it provides the supportive baseline for all interaction."[19] This is elegant logic; if descriptions

42

are to be made of movements which are essential to the culture, it can by extrapolation describe something essential about the nature of one of the performed arts, when such movements are found in the dance. "When we discover similarly structured bits or phrases of movement redundantly used in dance and in everyday life, we feel confident that we have found stretches of movement that form a basic part of the movement style of the culture."[20] They describe those movements, "characteristic stances and modes of using energy that underline all social interaction, all work and all activity in a particular culture."[21]

The conclusions of Choreometrics reaffirm and give firm evidential support to the notion that art is an essential part of life patterns, and that the reciprocal cross-feeling between the two is abundant. What is most impressive about this study is that it attempts to deal not with a single phenomenon, but a dynamic relationship of exchange, and that it describes this relationship in clear structural analyses. "The relationship of life to art forms the bond between the artist and his audience, though the specific terms of the bond have been mysterious until now."[22]

It is simplistic to assume that Choreometric parameters can only explain the most direct replications of dance and everyday activities. Choreometrics is observing a fundamental and basic shared behavior, the continuum which ties an art style and a life style together, illuminating one of the ways in which performance shadows and forecasts underlying social structures. If the performed arts, as represented by song and dance, are the most condensed and crystallized expression of a people, then by looking at performance, we can be informed about the society. This view gives weight and a different perspective about connections between art and life; it uses art as the measure of society.

Pleasure in performance can come through a sense of recognition set up by the rippling of internal associations. There is a shared experience between the artist and his audience -- at some level. "I think that whenever you take something you know very well and vary it, this in itself yields pleasure. To the extent that the variation becomes more and more discrepant, and at the same time remains true to the original behavior, the degree of interest and pleasurable arousal increases."[23]

These associations, no matter how individual, are shared -- at some behavioral interface -- by the cultural group surrounding the individual. Cantometrics, Choreometrics, micro-kinesic analysis, interactional kinesic observations -- all these disciplines are trying to uncover the nature of that relationship.

An understanding of the Choreometric principles and the application (in general or specific terms) of its structural analytic methods, can greatly enrich the viewing and making of performances. With that enrichment and the knowledge that goes with it, much can be discovered about the forms, structures and interconnections that exist in art and society -- both in our own culture and in others.

NOTES

1. Michael Kirby, "Criticism: Four Faults," <u>The Drama Review</u>, September, 1974, (T-63), pp. 62, 66.

2. Richard Schechner, "TDR Comment: A Critical Evaluation of Kirby's Criticism of Criticism," <u>The Drama Review</u>, December 1974, (T-64), p. 116, 117.

3. Conrad M. Anensberg, "Cantometrics in Retrospect," <u>Folk Song Style and Culture</u>, Alan Lomax and staff. American Association for the Advancement of Science, Washington, D.C., (Publication no. 88), p. 301.

4. Alan Lomax, "Choreometrics and Ethnographic Filmmaking," <u>Filmmakers Newsletter</u>, v. 4, n. 4, February 1971, p. 23.

5. Alan Lomax, "The Stylistic Method," <u>Folk Song Style and Culture</u>, op. cit., p. 7.

6. Alan Lomax, "Choreometrics and Ethnographic Filmmaking," <u>Filmmakers Newsletter</u>, op. cit., p. 26.

7. <u>Ibid.</u>, p. 25.

8. Alan Lomax, Irmgard Bartenieff, Forrestine Paulay, <u>Sonderdruck aus Research Film</u>, v. 6, n. 6, 1969, p. 510.

9. Alan Lomax, "Choreometrics and Ethnographic Filmmaking," <u>Filmmakers Newsletter</u>, op. cit., p. 33.

10. <u>Ibid.</u>, p. 26.

11. <u>Ibid.</u>, p. 24.

12. Alan Lomax, "Toward an Ethnographic Film Archive," <u>Filmmakers Newsletter</u>, op. cit., p. 33.

13. <u>Ibid.</u>, p. 4.

14. Alan Lomax, Irmgard Bartenieff, Forrestine Paulay, "Dance Style and Culture," <u>Folk Song Style and Culture</u>, op. cit., p. 226.

15. Alan Lomax, "Choreometrics and Ethnographic Filmmaking," <u>Filmmakers Newsletter</u>, op. cit., p. 26.

16. Ibid.

17. Ibid., p. 23.

18. Daniel N. Stern, "On Kinesic Analysis: A Discussion with Daniel N. Stern," (interview) The Drama Review, September, 1973, (T-59), p. 120, 121.

19. Alan Lomax, Irmgard Bartenieff, Forrestine Paulay, "The Choreometric Coding Book," Folk Song Style and Culture, op. cit., p. 262.

20. Ibid., p. 228.

21. Ibid., p. 229.

22. Alan Lomax, "The Stylistic Method," Folk Song Style and Culture, op. cit., p. 6.

23. Daniel N. Stern, op. cit., p. 125.

THE CREATION OF AN ENSEMBLE PIECE

JOSEPH HART

This is an account of the development and production
of an ensemble piece, Wiglaf: A Myth for Actors.
It is in four parts. The first part presents the myth
which was the basis of the piece; the second describes
the process of bringing the myth to life in production;
the third describes the performance as it evolved; and
the fourth is an account of the exercises used by the
writer/director with his company in the process of
realizing the myth on the stage. Ed.

WIGLAF: THE TEXT

Old Wiglaf was a mighty king who ruled the North Lands of forests and lakes. He had been king for fifty years, and in that time he had pushed the borders of his kingdom beyond all song and memory. He had brought the faith of Christ to the North Land and forced out the old gods with fire and steel. To some he was Wiglaf the Great, or Wiglaf the Holy, and they told many tales about him.

One tale above all was sung and repeated, again and again, in many ways, and was never worn-out with the telling. It recalled how Wiglaf had stood beside Beowulf when the hero had made his last battle. Together they slew a great dragon which had guarded a treasure, and Wiglaf had spread the gold before Beowulf's eyes so the hero died glad in his victory. That was the fiftieth year of Beowulf's reign. Then Wiglaf had reigned for fifty years.

Now the time of Christmas was at hand, when fire and laughter defied the darkness, and the night wind carried the Advent hymns. The farm yards rang with the sound of axes and swords against holly and fir tree. The brimming mead cups spilled on the hewn oaken tables, and the liquor ran on the floor to hiss with the flames of the yule log. It was a time of peace and full bellies, and torches that burned until dawn. The legends of Beowulf were dinner songs now. The monster Grendel, and the Worm of the Horde were stories to frighten bad children, before a father would laugh and kiss them and put them to bed. This was the careless season of the Christ child's birth. The old gods were buried and far away.

But even as the days of the year were numbered, and the land was loud with the noise of the feasting, another sound arose on the wind. Like a great slow howl it grew in the darkness. Louder and stronger it gathered from every part of the kingdom. It challenged the hymns, and the laughter stopped. Now the bright mead halls were filled with fear and stories were whispered of a terrible Beast let loose in the North Lands. Farms were found burned and black in the snow. Orchards were torn and scattered like sticks. And the great stone walls of the mead halls themselves were scorched and battered, and bodies of guardsmen lay broken and dead. Some said it was Grendel come back from hell -- or a second dragon seeking its gold. Then the old ones remembered Fenrir the Wolf, the great foe of Odin. They said he had broken the bonds that were forged by the gods and was bringing the end of the world.

From all over the North Lands the people fled as the dark shadow grew. In one great voice they called upon Wiglaf.

And Wiglaf was enraged at their fears. He cursed their superstition in the name of Christ the King. Then he took up the weapons of Beowulf -- the sword and the spear, and the bow so strong only his hand could bend it. For years he had kept them, polished and shining and useless as relics. Then each one was blessed in the Trinity's name as he gathered his strongest soldiers around him. He would hunt for the Beast over land and sea. He would hunt it forever -- if forever were needed.

He was seventy years old at the time.

Far and wide Wiglaf wandered in the dark time of winter. Wherever he went were the signs of destruction, and the sound of mourning was the wind at his back. His heart filled with hate for the Beast who had ravaged his works.

But however far he marched -- or however hard the men pulled at the oars -- the great Beast always escaped them. No one they asked could tell where its lair was, and there was no one alive who knew what it looked like. The seasons passed by in frustration, and the year made its giant circle. The Christmas moon was rising again, and Wiglaf's sleep was troubled with dreams.

One night as he lay on the deck of his longship, he dreamed of the last fight of Beowulf. He heard the old hero roar out his challenge, and watched the silver dragon rear its head against the sky. He remembered the stench that made him vomit, and the fire that blistered his knuckles and cheeks. He heard himself screaming at legs that refused. Then he saw mighty Beowulf stumble. His beard was burned off and his lidless eyes bulged, and his heavy sharp sword was as weak as a reed in the hot yellow wind. Then Wiglaf remembered a sound that had never been heard in that age of the world: The hero was crying for someone to help him. Then Wiglaf's fear was broken. His young voice cracked on the note of a war cry. He flung his arms about Beowulf and pulled the old man to his feet. Then they stood there together, the young and the old, to meet the dragon's attack. Wiglaf slashed at the belly, as the great sword of Beowulf pierced up through the jaw and entered the brain. For a moment the head hung dead in the air, then dropped to the earth like a stone. The fire went out, and a breeze came to bathe them.

Then Wiglaf awoke. The breeze he had felt was the fresh air of morning, and he ordered his men to pull up the sail. He thought no more about Beowulf, but turned his mind to the hunt and the Beast he had never seen.

That night they dropped anchor in the cove of an island where a great forest stood above them, black against the stars. No map of the kingdom had charted this island, and no man among them remembered its name. But they warmed themselves with liquor and songs, for the night was bitter and they were far from home this Christmas Eve.

But Wiglaf was restless as he watched the dark trees and saw the white moon rising among them. He left his men to keep the ship, and went ashore armed with the weapons of Beowulf. He found a path that shone in the moonlight. It wound up from the shore and into the trees. As Wiglaf climbed, a figure approached and he heard someone calling his name. He drew nearer and saw an old woman, struggling under a great load of wood. He lifted the bundle from her shoulders and laid it on the ground. She was very old and one eye was missing.

Then Wiglaf said, "As I came up the path you were calling to me. How did you know my name?"

The old woman smiled and answered, "Who could live as long as I have lived and not know the King of the North Lands?" Then she told him many things about himself, and he wondered at her knowledge.

"What is your name?" Wiglaf asked her.

But the old woman ignored his question. Instead, she said, "You have come to the Island of Fenrir the Wolf, where the old ones say he was bound by the gods and will break loose some day to ravage the world."

These words made Wiglaf angry, and for a second time he demanded her name. But again the woman ignored him and said, "The trees are called the Forest of Odin, for the old ones say that he hung for nine days and nights on the tree Yggdrasill to learn all manner of knowledge for man."

Now Wiglaf was exceedingly angry at the sound of the heathen names, and for a third time he demanded the old woman's name. But she only smiled at him and answered, "It is no wonder you do not know me. It is many years since Wiglaf made me an exile."

A light seemed to shine in her one good eye. Then Wiglaf knew he had seen her before -- but so long ago he could not say where.

"I am an exile," the old woman said. "Each evening I gather the wood of the ash tree, Yggdrasill. The old ones say the roots of that tree reach down through the world. At its base is the pool of Mimir where Odin drank to gain knowledge for man, and paid the great price with one of his eyes. But that was long ago," she smiled. "Now I warm my feet on the World Tree's branches."

But Wiglaf would have no more of such talk. "I hunt for the Beast who has ravaged my land," he said. "Tell me if his lair is here!"

"The Beast is here," the old woman said. "Go home before you find him."

Then Wiglaf was wild with rage and lifted his sword to strike. But the old woman straightened and raised her hand and her voice was as sharp and as strong as a man's.

"Put up your sword," she commanded. "You cannot kill me. You have only the power to banish me. Three times you have asked me my name. I have many names for those who remember. But for you, great King and hunter, let my name be Doubt!"

The word ran like an echo among the trees, till the whole forest whispered the name. Then Wiglaf stepped back and lowered his arm. He cursed the old woman in the name of Christ and hurried past her up the path. But she called to him again, and now her voice was as old and as soft as before.

"You have helped me with my burden, now I will help you with yours." She held out a long staff of ashwood and urged him to take it. "To some it is sacred to Odin," she said, "but it helps any traveler to walk in the snow, or it serves as a weapon when all others fail."

Wiglaf paused a moment before he took it. Then without a word to the woman, he turned and entered the forest.

Into the forest went the King of the North Lands, guiding his steps with the ashwood staff. He raised his voice in a song of praise, and called on Christ and the Virgin to help him. But silence and cold were the forest's answers, and his thoughts went back to the old woman's words. Then a little wind came and scattered the snow drifts, and blew the cold crystals in Wiglaf's eyes. His vision blurred and the images ran. He saw dark movements among the trees and he stopped and called out his challenge. Three gray wolves moved forward to meet him. Their eyes were as bright as little blue flames and the mouth of each was a wet red grin.

"Where are you going?" they whispered to Wiglaf. The words of the three were a fugue of fear. "Where are you taking your weapons, great King?" Then Wiglaf stepped back and drew out his sword. The long blade gleamed in the light of the moon.

"I hunt for the Beast who has ravaged the North Lands. I come in peace to all other creatures. Tell me where I may find his lair."

Then the gray wolves laughed and snapped at the air, and moved to make a circle around him. "Yes," they snarled, "we will answer your question. But first we must feast and bring you to dine!" With a roar the three rushed upon him, but Wiglaf stood ready to meet the attack. A single blow sliced open a skull, and Beowulf's sword flew among them like wind. Then a cold mist came down to cover his eyes, and Wiglaf watched in wonder as the world around him changed.

He was a young man again in the spring of the year on the day of Beowulf's death. The dragon's carcass lay steaming around him and his hands were full of the treasure it guarded. He faced the three soldiers who had fled from the challenge, and left the old hero to fight all alone. They were good men and brave fighters who had won many battles, but they had no heart for the dragon's flames. So Wiglaf cursed them and bragged of his valor, and showed them the treasure he claimed for his own. Then the men were angry at the shame he put on them. Out of spite they called him a liar. It was Beowulf who had witnessed his deeds and Beowulf was dead. They mocked him for his youth and the courage of his tongue, and Wiglaf's cheeks were red with anger.

"More than the treasure," he shouted, "I claim the Kingdom

too! The King is dead and I have won his crown!"

The the older men laughed and made jokes to his face. They said he should wait for his whiskers to grow, or until he had known his first woman. Then one of them said, "He's both liar and thief. Let us take the gold and divide it ourselves." All three agreed and moved forward to take it.

But Wiglaf flung the gold in their faces, and before they were ready he struck with his sword. One man was killed, and another was crippled, and the third lay bleeding and begging to die. Then Wiglaf stripped them of weapons and clothing, and made them crawl naked from the point of his sword. "I am King now," he cried, and the hills of spring answered, and the world was full of his laughter and strength.

Then the mist left his eyes and old age returned. He was alone in the forest, and the stillness of night was around him again. The gray wolves were gone and the snow held no sign of them. But the great sword of Beowulf was nowhere to be found.

Deeper into the forest went Wiglaf, lifting his voice to Christ and the Virgin. But the song of praise had become a command, as he called on heaven to show him the Beast. The ashwood staff was his strength in the snow.

He stopped when he heard a sound behind him. Again there was movement among the trees. He weighed his heavy spear in his hand, and called out a challenge that shattered the air. A doe stepped into the moonlight before him. Her eyes were warm and her words were a song like the sound of a harp.

"Where are you going?" she asked him. "Where are you taking your weapons, great King?"

"I hunt for the Beast who has ravaged my land. Tell me where I may find his lair." There was silence again, and the doe only stared at him. Then Wiglaf spoke harshly. "I come in peace to all other creatures."

The doe bowed her head and picked her steps slowly. "I know of the Beast, and where you will find him. But I never shall answer your question, O King." Then she leaped away and began to run.

But Wiglaf hurled the heavy spear after her. It pierced her body and dragged her down. A terrible groan escaped from her throat. It ran louder and louder among the trees, till it seemed the whole forest was writhing in pain. Then as Wiglaf watched, the groan turned to laughter and the doe rose up, no longer a doe. Once again the forest was changing around him. He was young again and the season was summer.

Before him stood the fairest woman his eyes had ever seen. He watched her transfixed. She moved like the breeze made visible, and her soft voice spoke of unimportant things. She was the daughter of a line of many kings, and Wiglaf wanted her for his wife. But his words were coarse and clumsy and he blushed whenever she laughed.

She moved like the breeze made visible, and he was sick with desire for her.

She challenged him with her father's great wealth, and Wiglaf answered with tales of his own. Then she told of her father's lands and Wiglaf spoke of the size of his own. So the two made a contest of wealth and possessions. Whatever she said he would answer in kind. And each looked for some way of besting the other. And all the while that he watched her his great desire grew.

At last she said, "I have a possession you cannot match." Then she teased him to make her tell. Wiglaf was mad to know her secret, but she laughed and ran away. She ran through the bright summer flowers, and he followed, demanding to know. At last she turned and smiled at him. She said, "There is one thing I have you cannot match. It is bigger than all the others we bragged of. From the way you have watched me this afternoon, you do not have me, but I have you." Then laughing, she turned and ran away.

But Wiglaf followed, his heart in a rage. He caught her and dragged her down on the earth. She struggled to rise but his rough hands held her, and his hard mouth covered her screams. He tore at her gown until she was naked, and pressed her flesh with his own. Then he opened her body and broke her, and she screamed with pain in his ear. "I have made your match," Wiglaf whispered, as the darkness came over his eyes.

When he awoke he was still in the forest. The doe was gone and no blood marked the snow. But the great spear of Beowulf was nowhere to be found.

So Wiglaf ran through the forest, shouting his prayers at Christ who was deaf. The great forest smothered his voice in its silence, and silent eyes watched the king as he ran. He paused for breath at the base of an oak tree. The cold air was burning and tearing his lungs. Above him a voice cried down through the branches.

"Where are you taking your weapons, O King?"

Wiglaf stepped back. It was the voice of a raven hidden high in the branches, squatting against the round white moon.

"Where are you taking your weapons?" she asked him.

"I hunt for the Beast who has ravaged my land. Tell me where I may find his lair. I come in peace for all other creatures." So he answered, and fixed the string to his bow.

Then the raven said, "From where I sit I can see the whole forest. I know the Great Beast and where you may find him. But never ask me to tell for I never will say."

Then the words made Wiglaf angry and he threatened the bird with his bow. But the raven fluttered from branch to branch, spoiling his aim in the tree's dark hair. Then Wiglaf struck sparks at the base of the oak tree and fire ran up its dry, naked sides. The raven screamed as the fire reached up to her. She plunged from the branch to fly and escape. But Wiglaf's arrow struck deep in its mark. Her breast burst open and the blood poured down. It spilled over Wiglaf's forehead and face. It matted his hair and blinded his eyes. He dropped the great bow and fell to the ground. But the ground that he touched was barren of snow.

He wiped his eyes. It was water, not blood, that ran on his hands. His vision cleared slowly. Around him he saw the rich time of autumn, and a priest stood above him pouring waters of faith. This was the time of the Great Conversion, when Wiglaf brought Christ to the North Lands. Among all his people he traveled, bending their will to his own. Many came gladly, as Wiglaf had done. In that rich time of autumn he gathered a harvest for Christ. Then he came on a priestess who tended a fire sacred to Odin. She refused the water of faith that he offered and covered her ears at the gospel he preached. A great crowd gathered to witness their struggle. Then the priestess turned to the people and said, "Odin speaks to me, he tells me his will. He challenged this Christ to wrestle with him, but Christ never came. If Christ exists then Christ is a coward!"

Then a murmer of doubt began in the crowd. But Wiglaf answered the priestess, "If Odin exists then Odin will save you!" Then his men cast the priestess into the fire. They held her down as her screams tore the air. Her flesh fell away, stuck to pieces of clothing. Then they lifted her up on a high wooden cross. The people would see her and all were afraid. And Wiglaf shot an arrow that split her heart in two.

The North Lands were all converted that autumn.

Then the vision passed and Wiglaf stood in the midst of the forest. There was no trace of the tree or the raven. There was no mark of blood on his hands. And the great bow of Beowulf was nowhere to be found. He had only the ashwood staff in his hands. For the first time in all of his journey, Wiglaf felt old and afraid. He began walking slowly, straining his eyes to find his own footprints. He lifted his voice in a song of prayer. But the words were a whisper and the names were confused. He prayed both to Christ and to Odin, and the forest repeated the prayer. Then a shadow stood up in the forest, and he stopped and watched as it came.

A great bear stepped into the moonlight and stood on its legs like a man. "Where are you going?" the great bear demanded. "And why do you trouble my sleep?"

Then Wiglaf answered, "I have hunted the Beast who has ravaged the North Lands. But I lost my weapons and must go back. I come here in peace for all other creatures."

"But you came too far," the great bear growled. "You have broken my sleep and now you must fight me. We will fight without weapons -- your strength against mine."

Then Wiglaf flung off the robe of his kingship, and he wrestled the great bear there in the wood. But his arms were no match for the bear's heavy paws and he fell with his face buried deep in the snow. Then his ears were filled with the roar of a battle. He looked up and saw armies where trees once stood. It was winter still, but the place was the North Lands, and Wiglaf was fighting for another king's land.

Across the field the two armies clashed, while bodies and limbs were piled up for burning. The armies were equal, the dead were the same, and not an inch of the ground was given or taken. Then the king stepped out from the enemy lines and raised his hand for the fighting to stop. He called upon Wiglaf to meet him in combat. "You and I will decide this issue alone. Our weapons are equal, so match me in strength. Let us see who will rule in my land." Then he stripped himself and waited for Wiglaf. And both armies wondered at the king's great size. He was strong and tall, and far younger than Wiglaf. But Wiglaf could hardly refuse.

So the two kings wrestled between their two armies, and time and again Wiglaf was thrown. Then the young king flung his great arms about him, and Wiglaf felt his last strength fail. His enemy squeezed him against his chest and the breath burst out of his lungs. But even as he held him Wiglaf's hands were free. He pressed his thumbs in the young king's eyes. He gouged the eyes from their sockets, and with a scream they fell out in his hands. Then he crushed the bleeding face to the ground and shouted for all the soldiers to hear. "This young man defended his kingdom well. I award him six feet of its soil!" Then his men broke out of their line with a cry, and fell on the foe like a storm.

But the cry of the battle was the wind in the trees. Wiglaf crouched with the ashwood staff on his knees. The great bear was gone, and the king's robe had vanished, and he knew he was freezing to death. Then he wept and shouted his curses at Christ and he cursed the Beast who had lured him so far. His thin voice rose and the whole forest heard it. The trees themselves seemed to murmer and pray. All around him the forest was moving. Like a gate, the branches drew open. The great Beast was coming to meet him. Wiglaf leaned on the staff and moved forward to see.

What he saw was himself staring back. It was Wiglaf's own image, but smiling and young. It was armed with all the lost weapons of Beowulf, and wrapped in the robe of a king. The sound in its throat, like an animal's panting, was the laughter of scorn in Wiglaf's ears. Then Wiglaf remembered the words of the one-eyed woman, and he knew the meaning of the visions he'd seen. But still he moved to challenge the Beast. His only weapon was the ashwood staff. The Beast moved to answer his blow.

Again and again Wiglaf struck at the Beast, but the Beast parried every thrust. For every move that Wiglaf made, the Beast made exactly the same. The mocking laughter grew until it rang among the trees. Then Wiglaf felt his strength fading, and he sank to his knees in the snow. He taunted the Beast to strike the last blow. The Beast only waited and laughed. Then out of his pain Wiglaf called upon Odin -- upon the Father of All -- to pity him now.

And then it was that Odin listened and sent new strength to the King. It ran through his arm from the staff of the ashwood. It warmed his heart for a final attack. He struggled to his feet and raised the staff like a spear. With a cry he hurled his weapon, and the Beast did even the same. Both weapons flew and struck deep in their mark. Both hunter and hunted were wounded to death.

The dying Beast roared and the great forest trembled, and Wiglaf praised all the gods in their names. Then even as the two lay dying, a wonderful change began. The voice of the King and the groans of the Beast mingled till both were one. Then the words of the King became the cries of the Beast, and the dying Beast seemed to speak Wiglaf's prayer. And even so their bodies were changed. The form of the naked hunter was twisted to that of an agonized beast. And the form of the dying Beast assumed the grandeur of a king.

So Wiglaf the King lay dead in the forest. He lay armed with Beowulf's weapons and clad in the robes of his kingship. His face was young again, and fair, as if fifty years had been smoothed away.

In the first light of dawn the men came from the longship and found the two lying dead in the snow. And one of them said, "This was a beast as fierce as any that Beowulf slew." And a second one said, "Here are the marks of their struggle. In killing this beast our great King was killed. In this way too did Beowulf die." And a third one said, "Our good King looks so fair in death. So he must have looked on the day he helped Beowulf. And even Beowulf was not so honored by Christ in his death."

Then they lay Wiglaf's sword on his breast, and folded his hands on the blade. They carried him down through the forest and to the shore where the longship lay. And all the while they were weeping, and singing the praises of Christ for the wonder they all had seen.

There were others who watched them until they were gone. Then they came to the corpse of the Beast and raised it up on the ashwood staff. And the wolves and the deer were among them. And the raven was there, and the bear. They made the Beast a pyre, and they sang and they danced in Odin's great praise. So the animals made the Beast's funeral, and the dark forest rang with their revel. And far off at the oars of the longship, some heard the echoes deep in their minds.

It took almost a full year for <u>Wiglaf</u> to move from the page to the stage. This year of preparation was divided into two enormous "Acts," each four months long, with an "Intermission" of three months in between. Officially, the "Intermission" was for summer vacation -- unofficially, it was a time to study, plan and gather the final company of actors for the grueling day-in, day-out, rehearsals of the "Second Act."

The "First Act" began with a random group of fourteen student actors, gathered together in a theatre workshop course with the vague mandate to "explore techniques of ensemble acting." In a group as large as this, to which the only entrance requirement was tuition and some previous theatrical experience, the degree of talent and commitment touched each end of the spectrum. To some actors it was a total immersion in the experience, regardless of physical, emotional or social demands. To others it was a curiosity to be pressed later on in their scrapbooks of theatrical memories.

The "First Act" of <u>Wiglaf</u> ran from January to May, 1973, at the end of which the class performed their "work-in-progress" to a generally sympathetic but bewildered audience of friends and faculty. It took the form of an eccentric, staged reading, physically illustrated by the group. The presentation followed the text literally and in only a few moments, (the ship, the rape and the conversion scenes) did the theatrical metaphor replace the words of the text with conviction and clarity. The general consensus was that, as a show, <u>Wiglaf</u> was a respectable failure.

But "Act One's" real value lay far more in the difficulties and obstacles it uncovered than in its final unready product. It was during these classroom sessions that I found -- sometimes by accident, and sometimes by design -- the improvisational approaches, some of which I have formalized here in the section on exercises.

The main problem of "Act One" lay in the stripping away of devices, habits, "tricks of the trade," defense mechanisms, role-playing and the general academic reluctance to go beyond words, physical realism and the intellectual reservation that always asks, "What's the purpose of all this?" and "Can't we discuss it first?"

During "Act One" the exercises served the function of seducing the group into finding alternatives to their usual avenues of expression and relationships. <u>The Epileptic</u>, <u>Musical Head</u> and <u>Eternal Triangle</u> were presented first as games to ease the actors out of themselves and into the business of building a group. Gradually, as confidence and willingness to "take risks" grew, these exercises became structures which permitted each actor's personal expression. After a while I felt I could begin to make more specific demands on their developing discipline and trust. The Jailer and the Group Growth exercises were introduced as two more avenues to continue this gradual movement toward an ensemble sensibility.

Sometimes the studio seemed to explode with the energy of one mind, body and voice, rushing headlong wherever the impulse would lead. At other times the air was heavy with tension, inhibition, fatigue and resentment. The barriers were a long time in falling, and toward the end of "Act One" the group seemed rutted in the early stages of mutual awareness and trust.

Then, in one specific session, a massive breakthrough occurred and the group realized its potential for unity and commitment. It was at this session that I introduced the idea of The Conversion exercise. Since the actors were still so self-oriented, I thought that this single exercise might provide the perfect bridge to the fuller awareness we were fumbling for. It worked. As actor moved to actor, truly observing and reaching into the privacy of his partner's behavior, the group's momentum grew from release, to exhilaration, to spontaneous vocal music, climaxing in a joyous outburst, as fourteen actors were suddenly free to move, laugh, contact and respond as a single, sensitive unit.

The Conversion scattered the pessimism and gave the actors courage to attempt even a sketch of the myth of Wiglaf.

Throughout "Act One" we failed again and again, and came back again and again to try to build a group and confront the challenge of ensemble theatre. In addition to the exercises already cited, we borrowed freely, even randomly, from other sources -- Grotowski, Brook, Chaikin, Schechner, etc. We also spent hours in a local forest preserve playing games of The Hunt and observing nature both day and night for new perspectives to carry back to the studio and try out on Wiglaf.

In sum, "Act One," was a naive mixture of personal instincts, mistaken impressions, bright ideas, frustration, exuberance and the actors' own varying talents. Our massive hybrid of a showcase failed -- but the momentum for something more had begun.

During the months of "Intermission" that followed, the group split up, some actors leaving with reluctance, and others with a sense of relief, never to be seen in a workshop studio again. As both writer and director, I spent the summer of '73 immersed in the study of ensemble theatre, psychology and myth. Late in August the National Shakespeare Company in New York City offered the Workshop its Cubiculo Theatre and a spot in their season's schedule. Wiglaf was resurrected to fill the bill. This time the acting group was gathered by invitation and not tuition. It was to be a special project, working outside the normal academic schedule. The group was comprised of seven actors, a percussionist and myself. Late in August, 1973, we began the "Act Two" phase, determined to see

Wiglaf through to a rousing formal conclusion.

We worked on a day-to-day rehearsal schedule, each session averaging about four hours. We repeated, with increased attentiveness, the forest exploration, as well as beginning a program of continuous reading in Norse mythology and European folklore. (Many of the elements in our final production -- e.g., the use of the Old English language, the dragon's gold and the invincibility of the Young Wiglaf, were products of this research, just as other elements were the results of rehearsal experiments.)

The four months spent on "Act Two" were exhausting. The problems of the previous spring were still present, although easier to focus on in a smaller group. The old exercises of "Act One" were helpful in coaxing trust and building a sense of group responsibility. As time went by, specific exercises became obsolete and the group created its own spontaneous improvisations, whether in simple opening warm-ups or in exploring an episode of the myth itself. Also, the group began a concentrated and varied exploration of sound -- both vocal and instrumental. Throughout our rehearsals, the actors' movements and moods were constantly observed and interpreted by the percussionist. Several new exercises, helpful to vocal development, evolved spontaneously. (These too are explained in the exercise section. In addition, rather than trust to traditional musical instruments to express our work, the percussionist constructed instruments of his own that seemed to complement the various moods of the piece as he watched it develop.)

There were many pitfalls in this four-month "Act." I found both as director and participant that I had to watch constantly for repeated patterns, for objectives too glibly and "gracefully" arrived at, and for subtle demands by individual actors to shape the group to their own private will. This was more delicate and emotional work than the large rough-hewn task of the previous spring. The long rehearsal period opened up so many possible avenues that it was a constant chore to keep the main thrust of the piece sharply in focus.

As we worked, we followed a regular, but not rigid, rehearsal format. Normally, each actor would take a private half-hour to limber up, both physically and vocally. During this time I would watch for the "repeated patterns" and other things they had long since become "good at." Gradually, following these private exercises, the members of the group would extend their awareness to each other and the work would become more creative -- whether it was shared through imaginary "impulse exchanges" or actual body contact. Often the entire group would move into a single improvisation, sometimes extraneous to Wiglaf, but often yielding a spontaneous "group answer" to a reluctant problem in the myth. After a time, (the length of which depending upon the group's mood and energy level) we would gather in the center of the theatre space to work on facial and vocal muscles, and to concentrate specifically on the exploration of sound and making of our own "music." (The "music" of this circle together with the vivid memory of our local forest under the light of the full moon, would later develop into a vocal "metaphor" for the moonlight of the Raven sequence.) After the vocal exercises, we would occasionally talk over an episode yet to be explored, or read the myth aloud, in whole or in part, for fresh insights. Often I would assign the actors a specific format I had planned in private. Invariably, they would take the original direction and achieve a deeper, more definitive realization than I had anticipated. As we explored each episode of the myth, we often found the need to rearrange the text to suit our own unfolding theatrical metaphor. As each episode was realized to our satisfaction it became "set" -- loosely, yet firmly, bound to the metaphor which we had discovered.

Sometimes, for variety and surprise, I would re-introduce one of the earlier exercises to break the pattern of the rehearsal. What had originally been light-hearted or superficially exciting "playthings" would take on new dimensions. For example, The Magician, when led by a particular actress, suddenly uncovered a whole new dimension in female sexual power which was to lead directly into the final metaphor of the "priestess" scene. The Jekyll and Hyde exercises trained us for the transformations of the Old Woman sequence and the Group Growth exercise expanded to fill our theatre space and train us to maintain psychic contact throughout the changes of the various forest sequences.

Although "Act Two's" group was far more concentrated, ambitious, and individually talented than that of "Act One," certain old "ghosts" kept reappearing. The specialized training learned in dance and singing classes sometimes intruded its own rigid discipline into the highly personal work of our ensemble. Extracting these old, "dead" patterns was sometimes painful for both director and actor.

One formal discipline, however, was priceless in the success of our work. This was mime. One of our actresses was accomplished in the art, and our preliminary warm-ups would frequently include mime exercises. This acted both as a challenge to any member of the group who was in danger of becoming too glib about his physical expressiveness, and it was specifically responsible for the success of the "Christmas banquet" scene and the repeated use of weapons.

After a short time, under these intense "Act Two" conditions, the formal exercises I have included in this article were left behind us. And well they should have been. I had come to believe that, with enough practice, anyone can become "good" at anything. When an ensemble exercise is no longer a challenge, it must be discarded. The exercises were "starting points" for creativity, and in this lay their greatest value. But then, so too was the text of <u>Wiglaf</u> only a "starting point" for our final theatre piece. In the end, the production had a body and a life radically its own. The text had become a general plan, a foundation for our own interpretation and interpolation -- in short, for our group's own creation.

In the end, the "stage" experience was far more exciting than the "page" -- something we could never have anticipated a year before.

WIGLAF: THE PERFORMANCE

The Stage

The stage was a bare floor with the audience arranged "horseshoe" fashion on rising tiers around the playing area. There was no "set," except for one large, black platform against the back wall. On either side of the platform was a single step unit. The floor was painted a dark, earthy brown.

Off to one side, in full view of the audience, the percussionist sat, surrounded by an array of instruments -- drums, chimes, wood blocks, sand paper, sleigh bells, tambourines and castanets, etc.

The only props on the stage -- and the only ones used in performance -- were two five-foot wooden staves. They were fashioned from fallen trees, collected in a local forest where the group had spent many rehearsal hours exploring and improvising.

The Action   Prologue

The actors, four men and four women, file into the open area and form a large circle. They stand erect and "open," sharing eye-contact and a sense of mutual concentration. All are costumed in black leotards and tights, topped by a loose-fitting, soft, gray tunic. Thick gray-green socks, extending almost to the knee, are cut to form stirrups around their bare feet. One actor, the poet or "skald," of the myth is clad entirely in black. After a few moments, a spontaneous rhythmic movement begins in the group. The percussionist follows with a deep, echoing beat of the water drum. An actress begins to sing a simple medieval carol. To its repeated chorus, "Alleluia, alleluia," the group moves in rhythm into the opening scene of the myth. The skald takes up one of the staves and moves to his position among the spectators, high above the action. Throughout the performance he will sometimes narrate and sometimes participate in the action of the group. On stage, character roles begin to emerge. Five actors create the rhythmic image of the sleeping, hissing Dragon. Two other actors assume the characters of the old King Beowulf and young Wiglaf, his kinsman. To the ominous beat of the drum, they follow the trail of the "hunt."

The Dragon

With hands weaving, heads bobbing and tongues flashing in a single shared rhythm, the group creates the image of flame, smoke and writhing coils. A single actress in the center of the group acts as a focal point, and lends a distinctly teasing, feminine air to the metaphor of the dragon.

When he discovers the sleeping monster, Beowulf gestures Wiglaf aside and mimes the arming of himself with shield and sword.

(This encounter depicts the actual last episode of the Beowulf epic. The lines are spoken in Old English, the language of the original poem.)

Beowulf:	Draca! Draca!
Dragon:	(awakening and hissing) Wha bith thi nama?
Beowulf:	Beowulf.
Dragon:	Wha bith thi nama?
Beowulf:	Beowulf.
Dragon:	Wha bith thi nama?
Beowulf:	(enraged) Beowulf!
Dragon:	(repeating over and over in mockery) Beowulf! Beowulf!
Beowulf:	Wha bith thi nama?
Dragon:	(laughing) Beowulf!
Beowulf:	Foeta me!
Dragon:	(laughing in imitation of him) Foeta me!
Beowulf:	(shouting as he attacks) Wyrm!

There is no physical contact between Beowulf and the Dragon. In his first charge, Beowulf is struck to the floor by the sound-and-movement impulse of the group. In his second attack, he is struck again and nearly enveloped in flames. His scream for help brings Wiglaf into the fight. He drags away the wounded Beowulf, and sets himself as a shield between the dragon and his king.

Dragon:	(to Wiglaf, hissing) Wha bith thi nama?
Wiglaf:	(bravely) Wiglaf. (Wi - laf)
Dragon:	(feigning deafness) Wha bith thi nama?
Wiglaf:	(attacking) Wiglaf!

As the dragon is distracted by the sudden charge, Beowulf, with a final effort, plunges his sword through the monster's throat. The group seems to crumble in upon itself, hissing and twitching in the image of the dying beast. As the two men embrace in victory, Beowulf collapses into Wiglaf's arms. Wiglaf shows Beowulf the treasures of the dragon's horde, and together they ponder the riches. Before he dies, Beowulf, speaking in modern English, tells Wiglaf, "You are King!" Kneeling over the body of Beowulf, Wiglaf begins to mouth the word "king," slowly and with effort. He repeats it over and over as the other actors begin to echo the sound. As the word grows in volume and strength, the actors form a circle on the floor. The mood becomes light and joyous. All "roles" vanish into the circle, as the word "king" is transformed into "spring."

The skald takes up the sound and moves onto the floor. Using the words of the "myth" he relates the transition of fifty years, from the death of Beowulf to the final year of Wiglaf's reign. Around him the actors "pass" the names of each of the seasons in turn. In the sound of each season's name, they attempt to discover and share some aspect of that season's mood.

The Christmas Feast

As the skald speaks of the time of Christmas, in the winter of the fiftieth year, he mounts the platform at the rear. The actors move from their circle into a scene of greeting and joy. The group projects the image of a noisy mead hall and a drunken Yuletide feast. Roles of friendship, rivalry and authority emerge. One actress, in the part of a slave, sings a lilting carol as she mimes the act of attending the guests. Conversation is loud and spontaneous. Once again the language is Old English. Following his narration, the skald remains briefly on the platform looking down on the feast. Then he descends, staff in hand, and moves out of sight of the audience. A brief scuffle at the "table" is quickly settled by the Old King Wiglaf. (He is portrayed now by a different actor from the Wiglaf of the Prologue.) When his "guests" call upon him to tell a story to complete their entertainment, he announces the tale of Beowulf and the Dragon.

> (It was at this point in the group's
> preparation that the task of actor

and playwright literally merged.
The entire story was the creation
of the actor who told it. It was
funny, fantastical and wholly in
keeping with similar stories
quoted in the Beowulf epic itself.
It was a "fish" story, stretching
and embroidering the facts of the
earlier Prologue. It was spoken
in modern, colloquial English,
and it told of Beowulf's death and
Wiglaf's lonely fight against not
one, but three dragons, each ten
times the size of the first.)

As his "guests" cheer him on, Wiglaf slaughters the first dragon,
chases off the second (who was "so scared he put his tail between
his legs") and kills the third with a single blow. For good measure,
he bathes himself in the monster's blood, and, true to medieval
lore, this act makes him invincible forever.

(This last ingredient was to add an
unexpected and welcome dimension to later scenes.)

After his story, Wiglaf calls for music, and the guests perform a simple, energetic folk dance to the song of the slave and the
beat of the drums and tambourine. Then, exhausted and happy, the
groups break up into couples. They lie on the floor to sleep, make
love or laugh softly to each other. The slave's song changes to the
hymn, "O Come, O Come, Emmanuel," as the feeling of a deep
Christmas night settles over the "hall."
Swiftly and quietly, the skald reenters. His attitude is one
of pride and contempt as he moves like an invisible presence among
the guests. As the slave's song continues, he speaks softly to the
audience. He tells of the "terrible Beast let loose in the North
Lands." Suddenly, the peace of the hall is shattered. The guests
move in fear, peering over the heads of the spectators -- as if
searching the outer darkness of the winter night. A nervous rattle
of percussion follows their movements. The skald gathers power
and volume as he tells the tale of destruction. The guests cluster
around him in awe. Only Wiglaf stands isolated and unsure. The
skald calls up the memory of Odin, repeating the name to each of
the guests as he moves among them. Suddenly, the hall erupts into
a frenzy of pagan worship and prayer. The skald and Wiglaf "duel"
briefly across the space of the hall, matching the names of Odin and
Christ like swords against each other. As Wiglaf approaches in

rage, the skald turns his back, "vanishing" before Wiglaf's eyes. Laughing, he returns to his place among the spectators.

Through sheer physical strength and force of will, Wiglaf "reconverts" each of his guests. The cry of "Odin" turns to the penitent repetition of the name of Christ.

In command once more, Wiglaf calls for his robe and his weapons, using the Old English words for each. Once again the slave begins the hymn "Emmanuel." It is taken up by the entire group as the actors mime the arming of the king. The hymn swells to a militant chorus as they gather behind Wiglaf and the hunt for the "Beast" begins.

The Hunt

The skald narrates the passing year as the percussionist follows the action of the hunt. The Old English word for beast, dear (pronounced "dare") is called in challenge again and again. Slowly the group's confidence turns first to frustration and then to fear, as they gather around Wiglaf at center stage. Then he raises his fist high in the air and brings his arm down in a slow steady beat. To the deep, reverberating boom of the water drum, the group moves to create the sound and rhythm image of a plunging longship. Speaking above the noise, the skald crosses the stage and mounts the platform at the "stern" of the ship. His attention is riveted upon Wiglaf, but the king is oblivious to his presence. The skald's staff becomes the ship's "tiller" as he too joins in the rhythm of the group. The beat of the "oars" rises to a frenzy. Then, with a loud echoing cry from the throats of all, the longship "weighs anchor" in the cove of the Island-Without-A-Name.

The Island Forest

For a long moment the actors stand silent, their eyes searching for the "crags" and "forest" they project all around them. The cold stillness of midnight seems to seep through them, and the rolling of the longship at anchor becomes the slight, rhythmic swaying of their bodies.

Wiglaf moves among them, whispering encouragement to each. When he comes face to face with the skald, he stands transfixed for a moment, his back to the rest of the group, as the skald tells of Wiglaf's restlessness and his decision to hunt alone by the light of the moon.

Other actors move to fill the stage with the image of the

island forest. Each actor stands erect at some distance from the others. Vocal sounds are subdued and realistic, and all movement is restricted to slight adjustments of head, neck and face. Strict attention is given to the internal sharing of the "metaphor" with the rest of the group. The prevailing mood of the forest is one of silent alertness.

The Old Woman

As Wiglaf moves into the "forest" the skald descends from the platform. He passes silently among the "trees" watching the king. Suddenly he thrusts himself into the "body sign" of the Old Woman. He leans sharply on his staff, covering his right eye with a twisted hand. He mimes the carrying of a heavy burden of wood and he calls out to Wiglaf in a high, cracked voice. The dialogue of the scene closely follows that of the text. But the character of the Old Woman becomes a theatrical metaphor shared by the entire group. At each of the King's questions, her "body sign" passes to a different member of the company who answers him in the voice and manner begun by the skald. Throughout the scene, each actor, in turn, makes the abrupt transformation from "forest" to "Old Woman" to "forest" again. The angry, bewildered Wiglaf watches as the Old Woman seems to vanish and reappear among the trees. Finally, she reveals that her name is "doubt," and the word is passed in a sharp, hard whisper from actor to actor. Then the Old Woman "vanishes" and, for a moment, Wiglaf stands alone in the midst of the forest. As he starts to move off, the skald returns once more as the Old Woman. He offers Wiglaf the ashwood staff. Hesitantly Wiglaf takes the staff and moves away to continue the "hunt." The skald resumes his own character and returns to his place above the action.

The Wolves

As Wiglaf moves through the forest he begins to hum the tune of "Emmanuel." As if in response, a vocal impulse like the sound of a mighty wind passes through the trees. It rises swiftly trans-forming itself into the "group howl" of a wolf pack. Then, on shared impulse, the actors thrust themselves into the image of a running pack. They surround the King, starting and stopping sharply, to the rapid patter of the percussionist's drum. After a moment, three of the actors resume the forest image, while another three, still in the character of the wolves, turn their attention to the King. Wiglaf

66

mimes the use of his sword to keep them at bay. (Once again the dialogue of the scene follows closely the text.) The wolves dart in and out, their words tumbling over each other-like a fugue. When they attack, Wiglaf slaughters all three with his sword. As they die, their agonized screams are taken up by the rest of the group. The sound builds to a deafening roar all around Wiglaf. He falls to his knees, covering his ears in confusion and terror. Then suddenly, all is silent. To the beat of the drum and the words of the skald, the scene dissolves and transforms into the day of the death of Beowulf.

In one corner of the stage the three "warriors" nervously await news of Beowulf's struggle. In another corner, the Young Wiglaf mimes the act of bathing his body in the Dragon's blood. (The actors who portrayed the wolves have become the dead monster's steaming corpse.) An improvised dialogue begins among the three warriors. One of them (portrayed by a woman) accuses them all of cowardice. This evokes an angry response from the biggest and most powerful of the three. The third and most cunning of the group sides with the strongest against the accuser. As young Wiglaf moves into the scene bringing word of Beowulf's death, the three actors who formed the Dragon rise and move into sitting positions, each one facing one of the three sections of the audience. As the confrontation progresses they repeat the word "spring" exploring it through sound-and-movement, and acting as an accompaniment to the rising anger of the scene.

Wiglaf repeats the charge of cowardice but the cunning warrior accuses him of having murdered Beowulf and stolen his weapons. In answer, Wiglaf proclaims himself King. Then the strongest of the three challenges him to prove himself in combat. As Young Wiglaf struggles to manage Beowulf's heavy sword, only the actress hesitates to join against him. The cunning warrior works to persuade her. Finally she too joins the others in taunting Wiglaf to "prove himself." In a mimed duel, the warrior strikes a ferocious blow to Wiglaf's body. But the sword only seems to ring in the air as if it had struck against solid rock. A second blow brings the same result. The reverberating sound of "spring" and the ringing of the percussionist's cymbal, make the sword seem to tremble in the warrior's hands. Wiglaf is invincible, and the three are stunned into silence and fear. Then, with sadistic deliberateness, Young Wiglaf slaughters them all in turn as they beg for mercy or try to flee. His laughter of triumph over their bodies is taken up by the entire group. The actors move to resume the image of the forest as the figure of Old Wiglaf emerges once more. For a moment his laughter continues alone among the silent trees. Suddenly, realizing the delusion of his vision, he stops. He drops to his knees and searches in vain for his sword.

Wiglaf continues his hunt, muttering broken bits of prayer and hymns. His attitude is grim and determined. As he passes among them, the other actors merge together forming a broken line of bodies lying flat against the floor. Passing impulses of sound and movement, they form the image of a running stream. As Wiglaf pauses to mime the unslinging of his heavy spear, one of the actresses arises from the line. In the character of the Doe, she mimes the act of drinking from the stream. Wiglaf confronts her with the same question he gave to the wolves. In spite of her terror, she refuses to answer him. When she tries to flee, he hurls his spear and strikes her down. Her death moan passes among the actors on the floor until it seems that the earth itself is moving in agony under Wiglaf's feet. Suddenly the moan breaks off into teasing laughter. The image of the forest falls away as a new scene emerges.

Actors sprawl at random on the floor passing the word "summer" among themselves in impulses of sound-and-movement. Together with the percussionist they accompany the mood of the scene. As the skald speaks the words of the myth, the Doe is transformed into a beautiful, laughing princess, and the actor who plays the Young Wiglaf watches her in fascination. The dialogue of the scene is spare. The two move freely among the other actors on the floor. He pursues her, and she evades him. Several times he repeats "Marry me," and each time her answer is "No." At each object of wealth that he offers, she answers, "My father gives it to me." At one moment she allows him to approach and kiss her. Then she pushes him off with a loud "No!" and runs away laughing. The sound of her mockery ripples through the rest of the group on the floor. Angry and ashamed, Wiglaf makes his final offer. "Me!" he cries out. And again the answer is "No!" But Wiglaf continues to repeat the word, slowly and harshly, as the beat of the drum takes up the rhythm. Now the other actors begin to impede the princess' progress as she passes among them. Slowly, inexorably, she is caught in a trap of clutching bodies and hideous laughing faces. They seize her and lift her high in the air. They pull apart her legs, and thrust her open body into Wiglaf's embrace. For an instant all sound and action freezes. Then the stage explodes into a violent metaphor of rape. Male and female actors join in obscene rhythmic couplings, accompanied by their own wild shrieks and the savage rattle of percussion. As these abstract "extensions" rage around him, Wiglaf's own movements are realistic and brutal. On the platform above him a single actress externalizes the inner agony of the princess in her own personal "body sign." After a few moments, the frenzy subsides into the princess' long, slow wail of anguish. "Does your father give you that?" Wiglaf whispers, as he stands over-her. Then, cackling and twitching with obscene laughter, the actors return to the silent metaphor of the forest. Once more Old Wiglaf recovers from the vision, and searches in vain for his lost weapon.

The Raven

Wiglaf continues the hunt, speaking audibly to himself. The word "Christ" has changed from a prayer to an angry demand. The names Wiglaf and Odin seem to mingle softly with the sounds of the midnight forest. As he pauses a moment to search the ground, the actors cluster together in the center of the stage. As the skald speaks of the empty forest and the soft, bathing light of the moon, an eerie vocal music arises from their midst. After a moment an actress separates herself from the group and mounts the platform. Immediately she assumes the image and character of the Raven. At her sharp call to Wiglaf, the cluster separates, resuming the forest image and forming an illusion of distance between Wiglaf and Raven. Wiglaf repeats his previous demands and once again he is refused. The Raven appears teasing, petulant and even vain. (Together with Wiglaf's earlier dinner story, the Raven provided one of the two moments of humor in performance.) When Wiglaf threatens the Raven with his bow, one of the actors thrusts a quivering hand in front of the King's eyes, creating the illusion of the forest's concealing branches. Whatever position Wiglaf takes, the actor nearest him repeats the gesture as the Raven taunts and calls his name. At last, driven to frustration, Wiglaf mimes the act of striking fire at the base of the trees. The impulse of fire is taken and passed from actor to actor until the entire group seems to be writhing in flames. The fire reaches up to the terrified Raven. She is seized and carried forward as if in flight. Wiglaf's "arrow" strikes her down. As she falls, other hands reach out to press Wiglaf's face and cover his eyes. He sinks to the floor as the scene falls away and the group moves into the metaphor of the "Conversion" (described in the section on exercises).

Each actor falls into a rhythmic, "closed" body movement, repeating over and over the name of a particular god or goddess of Norse mythology. In working for a religious "conversion" it is Wiglaf's task to "open" each actor to full body freedom and transform the name of the old god into a joyous proclamation of the name of Christ.

At first, the "conversion" progresses rapidly, gathering momentum from actor to actor. But gradually, one actress emerges as a feminine counter-force to Wiglaf's masculine energy.

The god she invokes is Odin. As Wiglaf prays to Christ in thanks-
giving, she moves quietly among his "Christians" seducing them
back to Odin through the power of her own sexuality. In all ways
she appears as Wiglaf's total opposite, his repressed "anima"
spirit, and her appeal is to the darkness of instinct and sensuality.
In only a few moments she reigns over a writhing mass of sexual
forms, enslaved to the name of Odin. Her call to Wiglaf shakes
him from his prayers, and she laughs as every attempt he makes to
recover his people proves futile. For a time he himself seems
threatened by the powerful lure of the group. Slowly he moves to
join the "priestess" in a sexual embrace. Then, all at once, in a
burst of rage and sheer physical force, he bends her backwards, his
hands on her throat, strangling her. Her contact with the group is
broken and her power is shattered. The actors separate, each of
them suddenly racked with guilt and confusion. Then their shame
turns to fury as they seize upon the priestess and raise her up, her
arms outstretched in crucifixion. As she watches in terror, Wiglaf
slowly and deliberately notches an arrow to his bow. The bolt cuts
off her scream and she is lowered, quivering, to the floor. The
frenzy of the group subsides into mixed feelings of disgust and
enjoyment. Then Wiglaf moves among them quickly, abusing each,
and bellowing the name of Christ in their faces. Religious mili-
tance seizes them as the actors take up Wiglaf's cry of "Christ!
Christ!" They turn outward upon the spectators, and for a moment
it seems as if the same brutal "conversion" is to be loosed upon the
audience. But suddenly, at the height of the fury, the group fades
back into the image of the forest. Only the Old King, standing in the
midst of the stage, continues to beat the air with the cry of "Christ!
Christ!" When he realizes he is alone, he is stricken with fear and
scrambles to find his last weapon. But once more his search is
futile. Leaning on his ashwood staff, and mumbling incoherently, he
searches for the pathway back to his ship. On the far side of the
stage one of the actors slowly moves into the image and character of
the Bear. Wiglaf freezes in terror as the big animal lumbers toward
him.

The Bear

      The Bear booms out his challenge to the cowering King. Wiglaf
retreats, mumbling pleas and excuses. At last forced to stand and
fight, he mimes the flinging away of his royal robe. The Bear's
light slap sends him sprawling. In a second attack, he is lifted high
in the air and lowered in slow motion over the Bear's back, head
first, to the floor. As he falls, the rest of the group begins to move
in slow, sharp military patterns. As the drum follows them,

increasing its tempo, the actors march in furious precision, accompanying themselves with the sharp, rasping sound of the word "Winter - winter!" The sound and movement builds to a climax and erupts into a furious scene of battle. The actors rise and fall, filling the space with invisible foes and the clash of weapons. As the chaos rages, the young Enemy King (the same actor who portrayed the Bear) moves to confront the Young Wiglaf. With a loud echoing call, he silences the battle and boldly declares his challenge. As the two kings prepare to wrestle, the rest of the group sprawls in a ring around them. They cheer the opponents on with cries of "Win! Win!" Twice Wiglaf rushes the King and twice he is flung to the ground. The cry of "win" becomes joyous for some and desperate for others. At the third encounter the King lifts Wiglaf high off the ground in a crushing "bear-hug." But Wiglaf plunges his thumbs into his enemy's eyes, and the screaming King sinks backward to the floor. Now the sound "ter" is passed and repeated through the group as Wiglaf tortures his helpless foe. The syllable completes the season's name and the sound reflects the moment of horror. When the young King is dead, Wiglaf shouts his triumph and the group explodes into the image of war. Then, just as abruptly, the moment dissolves, and the group returns to the final image of the Island Forest.

The Beast

Old Wiglaf kneels alone, freezing and desolate, deprived now even of his robe. The names of Odin and Wiglaf are clearly heard in the sounds of the trees around him. Again and again he shouts for the "Dé-ar" to show itself. Then one at a time, each of the animals he has killed or fought emerges from the forest. They surround him and taunt him, repeating the word "Dé-ar, Dé-ar" like an echo to his cry. In agony, he blasphemes against Christ and calls out to Odin. In his eyes the figure of the skald, standing elevated and alone above the spectators, has become the image of Odin himself. He looks down on the naked King with a silent smile of power and contempt. As Old Wiglaf pleads, "Show me the Dé-ar!" the actor who has portrayed the Young Wiglaf throughout the story takes up the second staff from the stage. At a gesture from the skald, the Old King turns and faces his younger self. The sound, "Dé-ar, Dé-ar" turns to laughter as the "animals" pass around the two and move to the top of the platform. Gathering together, the actors form a group configuration, exploring in sound and movement the name "Yggdrasill," the Tree at the Center of the World.

Skald:	It was Wiglaf's own image, young again and strong. He was armed with all the lost weapons of Beowulf and wrapped in the robe of a king. And this was the Dé-ar he had hunted so long.
Young Wiglaf:	(aggressively) Wha bith thi nama?
Old Wiglaf:	Wiglaf

Three times the Young King repeats the question, and each time the answer is the same. Then the Old King asks, "Wha bith thi nama?" and again the answer is, "Wiglaf." Their frustration mounts as each seems to be mocking the other. Then the two, moving like mirror images, strike a vicious blow with their staffs. But the staffs never touch. In mid-air they seem to meet an invisible barrier, realized by a single vibrating sound from the percussionist's cymbal. Bewildered, Old Wiglaf strikes again and again at his "mirror" to no effect. Finally, he drops to the ground in exhaustion. Once more he turns to the skald. Humbly and softly now, Old Wiglaf prays to Odin to give him honor in death. As the skald speaks the words of the myth, new strength returns to the arms of the King. He turns the point of the ashwood staff against his own body. Then, in two sharp, violent movements, he thrusts himself upon it forcing his "mirror" to do the same. Impaled upon the staff, the image of the Young Wiglaf crumples into the form of a dying animal. The Old King watches in triumph over the death of his "Beast." The two sink to the ground and are still. For a moment they lie side by side as the only sound is the whispering of the World Tree's branches. Then, to the sharp demanding ring of the percussion, the two forms "exchange" their identities. The image of the dead Beast becomes the body of the Young Wiglaf, and the corpse of the dead King twists into the form of the fallen Beast.

Epilogue

As story teller, the skald moves onto the stage and stands over the corpses. He takes up the staff lying nearest the Beast, and tells of the coming of the Christmas dawn. The others, portraying the men from the longship, descend from the platform and gather around the bodies. The skald moves to the top of the platform as the group silently enacts the scene of discovery. As the skald relates the moment, the men take up the body of Young Wiglaf and the hymn

"Emmanual" begins as a quiet dirge. They carry the body with dignity, moving slowly around the perimeter of the stage. As they pass beneath the skald, he tells of the "Other eyes that watched the men as they passed." The group halts, still singing, as the skald descends the platform and steps sharply into the character and voice of the Old Woman. Approaching the body of the Beast, he touches his staff to its heart and whispers, "Dé-ar, wha bith thi nama?" He repeats the question with growing power and volume. Slowly the image of the Old Woman transforms to that of the god Odin as the Beast awakens to his demand. The Beast rises, struggling to form an answer in the sound-and-movement metaphor of his body. Finally, the word "Doubt" breaks through into the actor's personal body "sign." The "sign" becomes louder and clearer as the actor takes the staff offered by the skald. As the skald moves off the stage, he keeps repeating his question in louder and harsher terms. To the accompanying boom of the water drum, the answer comes back, "Doubt... Doubt...." The sound and rhythm of the group drives to a thunderous crescendo. Then, to the savage rattle of the drums, and the long echoing call of "Doubt," all lights are extinguished and all action stops.

A scenario account of the product of eight months work is at worst a worthless exercise in typing, and at best a ghostly skeleton of what actually happened. Wiglaf, a Myth for Actors, was presented only five times -- twice at Rutgers University and three times at the National Shakespeare's Cubiculo Theatre in New York City. Much of the material in the original text was omitted or re-structured. Despite the long hours and intensely personal rehearsal work, and despite the enthusiastic reception by the spectators, the group agreed that even more time and exploration could have been used. The group concluded that their work on Wiglaf could never be considered "finished." And there was a general recognition that no work in ensemble theatre ever really is.

WIGLAF: THE EXERCISES

During the rehearsal period the group tooks its preparatory exercises from many sources, in some cases borrowing literally, while in others, varying certain exercises to suit their own particular needs.

Occasionally the ensemble invented and gave names to exercises of its own:

1.   The Epileptic

The individual actors find a private space, clear of any
obstacles or protrusions which could cause injury. Then, at
the cue from the director, the actor releases his body into
total chaotic movement. All pattern of repetition is to be
avoided. The actor must, quite literally, throw his entire
body into a fit of broken, shivering, spontaneous movement,
making no effort to keep to his feet or protect himself.
After sixty seconds the director calls a stop and the actor
seeks total relaxation from whatever position in which he
finds himself. The goal of the exercise is the release of tension and the erasure of all patterns of intellectual manipulation over the body's behavior. Beyond sixty seconds the
exercise can be exhausting, painful and even dangerous.
Limited to sixty seconds, it can bring relaxation, shake off
inhibitions and, when done at the beginning of the session,
awaken a new sense of physical awareness in each member of
the ensemble.

2.   Music Head

The individual actor finds a phrase of music or song and
hums it in his mind until he is thoroughly familiar with it.
Then he allows the phrase to seep into his limbs until his
entire body is a "moving picture" of the music-phrase. (If
his choice has been a song, he must in no way "act out" the
meaning of the lyric.) After a few minutes, when his pattern
of movement has become thoroughly familiar to him, he moves
into a sharing position with another actor who is involved in
the same exercise. The two are then side-coached to "complete" each other -- to adapt their movement to the movement
of the other while keeping the rhythm and tempo of their original music-phrase intact. The two actors will then become a
single unit of shared movement. This exercise is almost a
metaphor for the problem of acting itself. Each character in
a play must preserve his own personal identity even as he
concentrates on his relationship with another character. The
exercise can be extended to include the entire company as
one pair seeks to complete another pair, etc.

3.   Jekyll and Hyde

Each actor begins to walk normally, studying in detail the
movement of his entire body. As he observes and becomes
aware of his tensions and idiosyncrasies, he begins slowly

to exaggerate them into grotesquerie. The transition must be gradual, as it is an attempt to make a sort of obscene caricature of the entire body and its everyday manner of movement. When the actor has pursued the grotesquerie to the limit, he must begin his return to normality -- but slowly, concentrating on the transitions he feels in his body as it "returns." The same exercise can be done using the actor's everyday speech, by having him repeat a simple sentence while observing his own manner of speech as it passes from normal to grotesque and back again. The exercise has the effect of stimulating self-awareness, concentration and strict control of the actor's physical "tools."

4.   Group Growth

At a signal, the actors move "en masse" to fling themselves in a pile in the center of the floor. All keep their eyes closed and concentrate on the sensations they feel in the press of bodies around them. Then, slowly, always maintaining physical contact, and taking motivation from the impulses they feel in the rest of the group, the actors in the mass begin to "grow." The total concentration of each actor is on the contact felt with the rest of the group; there is no "leader." The actor tries to "read" the feeling of the mass as if in itself it were a single unit of which he is but a part. He concentrates on finding the rhythm and pace of the group's movement, and he insinuates his own body into whatever avenue will contribute to the growth of the mass. The entire group stays in physical contact until it reaches the limit of its expansion. Here it should linger awhile as each actor experiences his part in the fullest expansion of the mass. Then it may be dissolved or retracted, in which case the process of growth is reversed and the group experiences the sensation of "shrinking" as it slowly closes back upon itself. At all times the actors' eyes are closed. The exercise, if strictly done, contributes enormously to the creation of "ensemble mentality" in a company of actors.

5.   The Eternal Triangle

Two actors face each other sharing a single rhythmic body movement. A third actor, the intruder, studies the movement. When he is ready, the intruder presents an alternative body movement, trying to lure one of the actors away from his partner and into a new relationship. If this "seduction" succeeds, the actor who is left now becomes the new intruder and the exercise is repeated. At no time is physical contact allowed. This exercise will help the actor in "reading" the larger ensemble and adapting himself to its rhythm and mood.

6.   The Jailer

The actors work in pairs. One is the "jailer," the other the "prisoner." Using only two fingers of one hand, the jailer very lightly holds the prisoner by some part of his body. To the prisoner, the grip of the two fingers must be regarded as confining as that of an iron manacle. Using every free part of his body, the prisoner must pull and tug as if trying desperately to break loose. The jailer at any moment may switch his "manacle" to another part of the prisoner's body. The prisoner's response must be immediate as he feels one part of his body set free and another part confined. The jailer has no obligation to actually restrain the prisoner, but only to suggest by the pressure of two fingers what part of his body the prisoner is to regard as "bound." The prisoner has the double obligation of isolating the imprisoned part from the rest of his thrashing body, and never at any time to break contact with the jailer. The jailer, by careful observation, can "exercise" the entire body of the prisoner by varied and imaginative shifting of the manacle. The roles may then be reversed. For both it is an exercise in concentration, in the isolation of parts of the body and in strict fidelity to a physical task.

7.   The Magician

The actors work in pairs. One is the magician, the other the subject. The magician's body is regarded as totally possessed of magic powers. The subject's body is regarded as totally under the magician's sway. Throwing a magic impulse with any part of his body, the magician affects a response of equal magnitude in part or all of the subject's body. Side-coaching should emphasize the magician's use of his entire body as well as the subject's total spontaneous response to the power of the magic.

8.   The Conversion

(This was the Workshop's "biggest" and most demanding
improvisation, calling upon all the skills and intimacy of
the group. In its entirety, it served as one whole segment
of the final project.)

Each actor finds his own private area, in no way seeking
contact or even giving recognition to the other actors in the
group. Each actor then discovers a basic rhythmic movement and accompanying sound that expresses a negative
feeling in himself. The movement and sound pattern should
express no desire for contact, no warmth, no availability
for sharing. The movement-and-sound must be something
which the actor is capable of maintaining for a long period of
time if necessary.

One actor, the converter, is designated to move among the
others looking for a likely subject to "open up" and "bring
out" of his particular negative pattern. After carefully
"reading" a subject's mood, the converter tries to insinuate
himself, through movement and sound into the awareness of
the other actor. The means which the converter uses must
be careful and exact -- otherwise there will be no conversion,
or one which is forced.

When the converter has discovered the right means, he stays
with his subject until the two have managed to erase all ves-
tiges of the earlier negative pattern. Then the two continue
the task of conversion among the other actors. And so it goes
on, in geometric progression, until all the actors are
"released" and the entire group shares in the joy of its
freedom.

If this exercise is done honestly by actors who have nourished a sense of trust and affection in their work, then there
is no limit to the expression of release and unity that the
actors will achieve.

9.   Yammering

The actors cluster together in a tight circle, sitting or
standing, and one of them begins the exercise. The object is
to repeat a monosyllabic word ("you," "me," "her," "why,"

"what," etc.) as rapidly as possible, keeping each individual
pronunciation of that word clear and distinct at all times.
The usual form of the exercise follows that of a mock confrontation "scene," with one actor pointing at another and
yammering, "You, you, you..." as the second actor re-
sponds in an equally rapid staccato, "Me? me? me?..."
All the rest of the actors can then join in, yammering their
own monosyllabic words as they "take sides," "defend themselves," "pick on" somebody else, deny an accusation, or
"argue a case." Throughout the exercise the group must (1)
make sense out of the "scene" by listening to what is being
said, (2) create constant variation within the scene by inter-
jecting new words wherever possible and (3) keep the words
flying rapidly and clearly, maintaining the integrity of each
individual pronunciation. The exercise continues until the
director calls a halt. (In the experience of the Wiglaf group,
"Yammering" was always a pleasant and energetic way of
disciplining lazy vocal habits, passive facial muscles, and
training the communication capability of the group, as the
actors worked together to make technical and emotional
sense out of what, to an outsider's ears, probably sounded
like gibberish or the ravings of the insane.)

10.   Jazz Combo

This was a far more demanding exercise than the enjoyable
and deliberately "hammy" Yammering. As with Yammering,
however, this exercise probably works best in a small group.

The actors gather in the center of the theatre space, sitting
in a tight circle, allowing each of them clear visual and aural
access to the others. The director then points to one actor
and asks for "the first sentence out of your mouth." The
actor must respond immediately with whatever comes to mind
With equal immediacy the entire group must pick up the sentence and make "music" out of the words.

This is an extremely difficult exercise in that the song of the
group -- however improvisational -- must be the single,
harmonic musical expression of all the actors. It requires
highly concentrated listening, as well as a personal sense of
"risk" as each actor tries to find both his own individual
vocal pattern and the total vocal expression of the group.
The grammatical structure of the original sentence is irrel-
evant. The words may be used in whatever order the group

wishes. For this reason the exercise can be compared to a jazz combo's improvisations on a single musical theme.

As the group becomes more proficient at meeting the demands of the exercise, the director can increase those demands through side-coaching. For example, the director might shout out, "Now do it as a lullabye!" and the entire group will have to adapt the same words to the feeling of that particular musical form. (There are many other possibilities: spiritual, military song, opera, etc.) Each time the group must adjust both individually and en masse to the new form. Also, the director can act as "conductor," using hand signals to direct the group to be louder or softer, or to pick up the tempo.

(In working on Wiglaf this exercise was crucial. It opened the group to new avenues of vocal expression and trained each actor to listen for even the slightest change in the total expressions of the group. The metaphors of Forest and Moonlight would have been at best both stagey and shallow had it not been for the demanding vocal work of the Jazz Combo exercise.)